JAY CONRAD
ANTHONY HERNANDEZ

GUERRILLA MARKETING
SUCCESS
SECRETS

52 WEEKS OF MARKETING & MANAGEMENT WISDOM

Guerrilla
Marketing
PRESS
AN IMPRINT OF MORGAN JAMES PUBLISHERS

GUERRILLA MARKETING SUCCESS SECRETS

© 2007 Jay Conrad Levinson and Anthony Hernandez
All rights reserved.

Paperback ISBN-10: 0-9768491-8-6

Paperback ISBN-13: 978-0-9768491-8-6

Published by:

Guerrilla Marketing Press
An Imprint of Morgan James Publishing
1225 Franklin Ave. Suite 325
Garden City, NY 11530-1693
800.485.4943
www.MorganJamesPublishing.com

Interior Design by:
Megan Johnson
Johnson2Design
www.Johnson2Design.com
megan@Johnson2Design.com

FOREWORD
BY JAY CONRAD LEVINSON

Guerrilla Marketing Success Secrets simplifies the difficulty of running a thriving business. That's quite easy to say even though it's very hard to do. So how do Anthony Hernandez and I do it?

The same way a marathon is run, the same way a mountain is scaled, the same way an archeological find is uncovered: by breaking seemingly complex concepts into easily digestible pieces. Anthony is one of the few Certified Guerrilla Marketing Association Business Coaches in the world and I am the Father of Guerrilla Marketing, which has fully prepared us to craft this book.

This book is rooted in both the business principles I've invested a lifetime testing on businesses just like yours and with Anthony's coaching philosophy that bridges the gap between theoretical data and the real world action needed to obtain results. The philosophy here is simple: if any method isn't working, it's useless to keep using it and hoping for a different result. Doesn't work.

This book is not so much about learning as it is about unlearning some of the many myths and misconceptions that surround entrepreneurship at all levels. Most of these myths center around the concept of hard work, which really means hard struggle.

In this book, we ask you to forget about your efforts and focus on your results. Do that one thing and you will experience higher profits while putting in fewer hours. Shouldn't your business be about making you free to be and do anything you like? We sure think so.

Jay Conrad Levinson
The Father of Guerrilla Marketing
Author of the "Guerrilla Marketing" series of books

INTRODUCTION
WHY WE CREATED THIS BOOK

This book began life as a series of weekly articles written by Anthony and published by the Ashland Daily Tidings and other sources. As the weeks passed, Anthony began hearing from people asking for back copies. It took a little while, but it eventually dawned on us that a book compiling the articles would be a great idea. Since these articles appear weekly, it seemed natural to include 52 articles, or one full year of content. Jay and Anthony immediately seized on the idea of creating the latest Guerrilla Marketing book. We put our heads together to refine and edit the articles with the absolute latest guerrilla wisdom, and you're now reading the fruits of that labor.

We both love small businesses because by definition they are pieces of their owners' souls. Entrepreneurs represent some of the most positive, can-do, creative people we've ever met. It's a mix of passion and creativity unlike any other. Little pleases us more than seeing a healthy vibrant business — and little saddens us more when we see a tool for freedom becoming instead a source of stress and angst for its creator. Far too many small businesses fail, and the real tragedy is that far too many of them do so needlessly.

We want to change all that. We believe that there is no mystery to running a successful business. We are convinced that a business should serve its owner's needs, never the other way around. We know that if you focus on the results you want instead of what you think or fear it might take to get there, that you can go farther, faster, and with much less effort than you might dream possible. The best part is that the process of attaining all of this good stuff need not be difficult or mysterious. In fact, it can be both simple and very enjoyable and fulfilling.

What kind of results will you get from reading this book and putting the advice inside to work in your business? We can't guarantee anything. We can tell you that all of our coaching clients receive the same knowledge you're about to receive. One business tripled its profits while the owner reduced her schedule by

25 hours per week. Another saw its profits expand by 80% while requiring 15 fewer hours per week of owner involvement. What results will you get? Whatever results you want to get. It really is that simple.

After you finish this book, we encourage you to visit our Web sites:

- **www.gmarketing.com:** The online home of Guerrilla Marketing International and Jay Conrad Levinson.

- **www.guerrillamarketingassociation:** Connect with business experts (including Jay and Anthony) on coaching boards, in weekly teleclasses, online discussions, and more!

- **www.coachanthony.com:** The online home of Anthony Hernandez, Certified Guerrilla Marketing Association Business Coach. Visit the site and be sure to subscribe to his Small Business Success newsletter, which contains the articles that will continue beyond where this book takes off. It's free and there is never any obligation.

Read, unlearn, and then go do. You'll be glad you did!

Jay Conrad Levinson
Puget Sound, Washington

Anthony Hernandez
Ashland, Oregon

ACKNOWLEDGEMENTS

JAY CONRAD LEVINSON

Although acknowledgements are due to Jeannie Levinson, Amy Levinson and David Hancock, the most profound and heartfelt acknowledgements belong to Anthony Hernandez, the guiding force behind this book. Without his energy and vision, you would be holding in your hands a book of blank pages. Thank you, Anthony!

ANTHONY HERNANDEZ

This book and indeed my entire coaching career would be impossible without some amazing people who believed in and mentored me.

Jay Conrad Levinson has helped tens of thousands of businesses and I am forever grateful for his ongoing support. He, his wife Jeannie and daughter Amy are the driving forces behind Guerrilla Marketing International and three of the best friends and colleagues I could ever ask for.

Larry Loebig is one of the most gifted coaches and trainers I've ever met. His wisdom and guidance have helped me over the inevitable rough spots and have also encouraged me to practice what I preach and live my own dreams.

Thanks to the Ashland Daily Tidings and to the community of Ashland, Oregon, for publishing and reading the columns that inspired this book.

My dear friend Rose Wahlin helped me create the products that led to my meeting Jay and forever changed my life. I can't thank her enough.

My friends at University Toastmasters opened new doors for me by helping me develop and refine both my speaking skills and my message, gifts that will last a lifetime.

Many thanks to Erin Malmquist for her friendship.

Last but not least, a huge thank you to my wife Robyn and son Logan who love me for who I am and who always have my back. All of this is for you.

TABLE OF CONTENTS

BEFORE YOU BEGIN
GETTING THE MOST FROM THIS BOOK

This book contains 52 chapters, one for each week of the year. Each chapter averages about two and a half pages and is designed to be quick and easy to read. Could you read through this entire book in an evening? Yes, but we don't recommend it because you'll get a lot of information overload and wind up remembering and using little or nothing. The whole point of this book is to give you lots of things you can do to improve your business and grow your profits with ease.

The best way to accomplish this is to take this information in small chunks and give it plenty of time to soak into your system so that you can make a fully conscious decision what to use and what to set aside. As you read, you'll find what you learn falling into one of four categories:

- This idea is in use and is working well for you. In this case, congratulations! You're already a step ahead.

- This idea is in use but needs work. Read the chapter a few times and decide what changes to make. Your business will benefit from making these changes.

- The idea is not in use but should be. Start implementing it slowly and watch your business grow!

- The idea is not in use and is not right for you. That's OK, because we certainly don't expect you to use everything presented in this book. We do ask that you give each chapter careful consideration, though.

Most people will probably read this book from beginning to end but some may need some information sooner than later and decide to skip around. No problem. Here is a list of the topics covered in this book and where to find them:

Topic	Chapter(s)
Marketing	all chapters (read Chapter 1 to find out why)
Finances	all chapters, but particularly 2, 4, 9, 23, 27, 46, 48, 49, 50
Customer Service	11-15, 25, 26, 31-34
Management	all chapters, but particularly 16, 18, 21, 23, 26, 28, 37, 39-42, 47-49, 51
Sales	20, 26, 27, 29, 30
Productivity	22, 23, 28, 36, 38-43
Employees	35, 44-48, 51
Year-End	41, 42
Summary	52
If you need additional help	53

Here's wishing you success and profits. You deserve it!

WEEK 1
WHAT IS MARKETING?

Traditional business thinking tends to think of marketing in terms of specific actions such as placing a newspaper ad, a radio spot, a TV commercial, etc. This limited definition carries three major problems with it:

- Most marketing resembles a grocery list of random ingredients with no idea of what the meal is going to be. Imagine strolling down the aisles randomly selecting ingredients without knowing what you want for dinner that evening or to eat for the rest of the week, only that you are hungry. Sure, you'll wind up with some delectable edibles. You'll also wind up with an inordinately high percentage of stuff that you simply can't use for reasons of taste, allergies, lack of complementary ingredients, etc. Not too efficient.

- The second problem is that most marketing is all about "me", the seller. My products are so great. My business is so wonderful. Drop what you're doing and come on down to give me your money. The thing is, customers only care about you and your business to the extent that you can satisfy their needs and wants. Think about any purchases you make: Do you make them to satisfy yourself or the seller? Enough said.

- Third, we live in an instant gratification society where everyone wants everything their way yesterday — including marketers. But marketing is more like an apple tree than a magic bullet: Plant an apple seed and you must wait a few years to start getting apples — a few at first, then more as the tree matures. Meanwhile, you're constantly applying liberal doses of water, fertilizer, and love. Same with marketing. With apple trees, you can watch the seedling growing, the flowers opening, the fruits slowly ripening. With marketing, that process is invisible, causing many marketers to cancel or change their campaigns — and in so doing, uprooting the growing tree and starting the whole process again from scratch.

Here is a more effective definition of marketing. This definition has three parts:

- First, marketing is any contact with anyone on your payroll with any-one not on your payroll. This definition is as expansive as it sounds and includes everything from your advertising to how you answer the phone, your store's appearance to all five senses, your employee attire, your refund policy, your warranty, that sign proclaiming "We reserve the right to refuse service to anyone" — and those are only a few ex-amples. Try this simple exercise: Walk into any business you like. What do you see, hear, feel, smell, and (if they sell food or drink) taste? What message is all this sensory information conveying about this business and your place in it? In other words, what impression are you getting? Is this impression making you more or less inclined to shop and buy? Now go back to your own business and ask yourself the same question. The answers may surprise you.

- Second, marketing is a process, not a series of disconnected actions. For your business, this process has a beginning, a middle, and (hopefully) no end. We'll be talking a lot more about this process in future chapters. Stay tuned...

- Third and most important, most marketing is a straight line that begins with an ad and ends with a sale. Not coincidentally, most businesses fail. Is there a correlation? You be the judge. Meanwhile, we encourage you to think of marketing as a big circle. This circle starts with your product and service, moves through the initial sale, and ends with satis-fied customers who both give you repeat business and who refer other customers to you.

You'll be hearing a lot more about the power of repeat/referral business and how to build a marketing process in future chapters. Meanwhile, we'll leave you with this thought: Let's say the item in question is $100. Traditional marketing aims to complete that sale, pocket the $100, and start over with the next customer. But what if this purchase is one that is made three times per year for 20 years, and what if each customer can refer three more customers to your business? That $100 has just become $24,000! Which would you prefer? As Jay says, "straight-line marketing is a straight line to the bankruptcy courts!"

WEEK 2
YOUR MONEY OR YOUR LIFE!

This old movie house cliché hides a deeper truth: Money is life because earning money requires an investment of time, as your alarm clock reminds you each morning. What do we mean? Try this simple exercise: close your eyes and start counting off seconds. As you do this, consider the fact that each passing second is gone forever. Each passing second is one second closer to the end of our lives as we know them. Tick tock, tick tock. The end keeps approaching, steadily and relentlessly. Tick tock, tick tock.

When we look at time this way, we suddenly realize that time is life itself. We further realize that any discussion about time and money must be a discussion about exchanging a non-renewable resource (our time, indeed our lives) for a very renewable resource (money).

What does this mean for your business? Traditional business thinking says that money is the engine behind successful marketing campaigns. This two-step approach forces you to invest time earning money for further investment in actually marketing your business. Question: Can you achieve the same results in a one-step process whose main ingredients are not money but time infused with energy, imagination, and information? Think you could do more with a lot less money? Think you might see faster results because you're investing time for the desired outcome instead of for some intermediate goal?

Remove the connection between money and effective marketing and you'll find yourself actually connecting with your customers and getting to know them as the wonderful people they are. You'll find yourself understanding your customers in ways you never thought possible, and you'll find that you're much better able to sense and respond to their needs. You'll also find your customers noticing and appreciating your human touch and returning to your business again and again. In nature, this is called a symbiotic relationship, where all participants benefit from their relationship with each other.

"Sounds good," you're saying, "but does it really work? Can the little guy with no money and no slick marketing program really triumph over the big guy?"

Jay tells the real-life story of Henry (name changed), who owns a small furniture store that happens to be smack in between two very large furniture stores. One morning, he arrived for work and was horrified to see that the store on the left had unfurled a huge banner: SALE — 50% OFF. Even worse, the store on his right had unfurled an even larger banner: ANNUAL CELEBRATION — 60% OFF. "I'm ruined," thought Henry. "No way I can match those deals with losing money on every sale. I can't even afford my own huge banner!" Then inspiration struck. Henry marched into the store and set to work. Within minutes, a much smaller banner appeared above his own door: MAIN ENTRANCE.

Who do you think was smiling all the way to the bank that day? Here's a hint: It wasn't the stores who spent lots of money on huge banners. What if Henry had gone down the money hole and slashed his own prices? He would have invested lots of money on his own marketing and confronted the prospect of a protracted struggle just to return to his starting point, older and, one hopes, wiser.

By removing money from the equation, using his imagination, and refusing to compete on price, Henry came out way, way ahead.

But what about the customers? Were they screwed into paying twice as much for their furniture? Not at all. Yes, the large banners attracted them to the stores. Yes, the sign proclaiming MAIN ENTRANCE funneled them into Henry's store. But nothing made them stay and nothing made them buy. Nothing, that is, except the confidence instilled when they found helpful knowledgeable salespeople, the superb selection of high-quality products, and the convenience of doing business with Henry. Had any of these elements gone wanting, these customers would have left the store to visit one of his larger competitors. Besides, despite the confidence, selection, service, and quality, not everyone who entered Henry's store bought there. Some decided that price was more important and purchased elsewhere.

In short, everyone got what they wanted and went home happy. Well, almost everyone; Henry's competitors weren't too thrilled. But hey, let's hear it for the little guy!

Why did people buy from Henry knowing they could save a bundle next door? Surveys consistently show that confidence, quality, selection, and service trump price with only 14% of customers citing price as their chief buying criterion. The other 86% seek wonderful buying experiences and are happy to pay a premium for it.

Question: How can you create a wonderful buying experience and how can you market said experience on a shoestring using your time, energy, information, and imagination?

WEEK 3
SOFTLY, SOFTLY

Window shopping is nice, browsing is even better. But actually forking over your money? That ultimate act of commercial faith isn't called "coughing it up" for nothing. Buying is a hard step made for emotional reasons that our rational minds are quick to second-guess. As if the actual purchase wasn't difficult enough, buyer's remorse sets in as you fret about whether you got a good value, wonder how you let the salesperson talk you into it, and dread getting the bill in your next credit card statement.

We can only surmise that everyone reading this knows firsthand what we're talking about. The kicker? If you're in business, then your very survival depends on getting people to take that hard step, preferably more than once. In a perfect world, the same people who take the plunge with you will convince others to do so as well since word of mouth is one of the most powerful marketing tools out there.

How can you increase your odds of success? Easy: Remove the sting from the buying decision by creating a series of soft steps that don't involve money or even selling. Each soft step seeks your customer's consent to take the next soft step and so on. The entire process builds trust and confidence and forges a relationship between you and your customers that eventually transforms the actual purchase from a hard step into yet another soft step.

Anthony uses the example of the classic children's book *The Little Prince* by Antoine de Saint Exupery. In one chapter, the prince meets a fox. This fox desperately wants a friend but is a wild animal that fears all who approach him. The prince asks how he can become the fox's friend and is instructed to visit the fox every day at the same time. During these visits, the prince is to do nothing but sit silently and watch the fox, coming a little closer every day. The fox explains that doing this will not only lessen his fear but will make him start to anticipate the pleasure of the prince's company. Eventually, the prince will draw near enough to touch the fox, who will then be tame. In other words, the soft steps of drawing nearer will eventually make the hard step of reaching out and connecting that much easier. We love this story because it encapsulates what marketing is about so beautifully.

What does this look like in the real world? Jay knows a summer camp in New York state that caters to affluent youngsters. This camp markets using small classified ads in relevant magazines and at trade shows. Does this marketing sell a camping trip? No. It simply asks people to send for a free videotape. The videotape arrives and regales prospects with images of gorgeous scenery, spotless equipment, superb counselors, and happy campers. Does this videotape sell a camping trip? No. All it does is ask people to schedule a free in-home consultation with no obligation whatsoever. Then and only then does the camp ask whether Billy wants to go camping.

Want an example of how not to implement your soft steps? Anthony and his wife visited a restaurant for lunch one day. As experienced diners, they expect to be asked about salads, drinks, etc. and usually appreciate the thoughtfulness. This time, however, their waitress bombarded them with questions and recommendations and dollar amounts throughout the entire meal. The food was good — they think — but they were too busy trying to take on fuel and get the heck out of there as quickly as possible to notice. Anthony would have complained — if only he could have gotten a word in edgewise. That was over two years ago and they have never returned despite passing the establishment regularly. Trust us when we say that high-pressure sales tactics are perfect for ruining the appetite.

So what about your business? What series of soft steps can you create that will make buying from you a pleasant experience that your customers will look forward to doing? Here are just a few ideas to get your creative juices flowing:

- Free samples. Prove how great your product is!
- Free lessons/demonstrations: Show your product and its benefits in action. Depending on your business, consider offering free lessons on how to use the product. Home Depot's free classes are great examples.

- Ironclad guarantee: Contrary to popular belief, the better your guarantee, the fewer problems you'll have with returns. Why? Because energy is contagious. Demonstrate that much faith in your product or service and that will pass through to your customers.

The basic idea is to create a process that gradually transforms prospects into customers by moving them from soft step to soft step, gaining consent at every step of the way. What will this process look like? That is where your time, energy, imagination, and information come in because each business is unique and there is no cookie-cutter solution.

WEEK 4
GEOMETRIC GROWTH

Traditional marketing focuses on linear growth by constantly seeking to obtain new customers. This chapter explains how you can get a far bigger bang for your marketing bucks by growing your business geometrically. Geometric growth consists of four elements that you can imagine as the four sides of a square. The good news is that it's far easier than it might sound. In fact, you're probably doing a little geometric growth without even realizing it.

The first element of geometric growth is to expand the size of each transaction. Restaurants where servers inquire about drinks, desserts, etc. and the piles of chotchkes near most cash registers are examples we're all familiar with. A couple more examples: If you sell clothing, you could recommend a sweater to go with the pants your customer selected. If you sell electronics, you could inquire about cables, remote controls, and more.

No matter what you sell, there is (or should be) an opportunity for the customer to upgrade. Likewise, there should always be a way for the customer to downgrade. Why? Because offering one item forces an all-or-nothing decision. On the other hand, if you offer the product you'd like to sell the most of in the middle of a range of options, you'll find that most people will indeed buy that product because it's neither ostentatious nor the "el cheapo" model. However, you'll find that a good number of customers will gladly pay more for the upgrade. You'll also find that a decent percentage can't or won't buy the middle solution but will opt for the smaller offerings. Just by offering a few choices, you've earned additional money from both the people who upgraded and the ones who would not have purchased otherwise.

The second element of geometric growth is increasing the frequency of each transaction. This works well for consumable products and for products that go in and out of style. Food and fashion come to mind. People who have purchased from you once have already taken the hard step, making future purchases that much easier. Practice fervent follow-up and you'll start seeing some familiar faces over and over again, far more often than you would otherwise. You'll also notice that your customers remain your customers for a much longer time.

The third element of geometric growth takes advantage of the fact that every customer is the center of a network of people. Word of mouth is one of the most powerful marketing tools ever invented. How do you tap into your customers' networks? There are lots of possibilities. How about two for one sales, bring a friend events, referral fees, catalogs, or coming right out and asking for the referral?

The fourth and final element of geometric growth is good old-fashioned linear growth. Every business needs new blood and yours is no exception.

As we said, chances are that you're doing a little geometric growth without even realizing it. This occurs because most marketing is done by accident. Think about your business. Do you do specific things that you consider marketing (such as running an ad in the Ashland Daily Tidings) and leave other contacts with your customers to chance? If so, we wonder how much more effective you could be if all of your marketing was intentional. Remember that marketing is all contact between your company and everyone else. If you lack a planned method of handing every such contact, then you are not taking full advantage of geometric growth. It's like driving a boat while dragging the anchor.

How powerful can geometric growth be? Let's say that your product sells for $100. The linear marketer would pocket the Benjamin and call it a day. Not the geometric marketer. They know that their customers need their products three times per year over a period of 20 years. They also know that each customer can refer three others. This $100 has just become $24,000 ($100 x 3 sales per year x 20 years x 4 customers = $24,000). Which would you prefer?

There is one huge catch, though. Geometric growth will be impossible unless you provide first-rate products and services and wrap that in world-class customer service that consistently under-promises and over-delivers. Furthermore, geometric growth is not for shuck-and-jive artists, nor is it about exploiting or milking your customers. In fact, it's about the exact opposite.

The road to successful geometric growth is paved with your ceaseless efforts to identify and solve your customers' wants and needs with absolute selflessness and integrity. It is lined with your commitment to quality and backed by your 100% guarantee.

Just how important are your customers? They are the only reason you're in business. No customers, no business. Lose your business and paying for such frivolities as food and shelter becomes that much more difficult for you. Sure, you may be able to get one over on them once, but are you in business for the short term or for the long haul?

WEEK 5
NANOCASTING FOR FUN & PROFIT

Common sense says that you should market to as many people as possible. We suggest marketing to as few people as possible. This is called nanocasting, which is the opposite of broadcasting.

Think about a TV commercial for any product. The commercial is a broadcast because it's going out to everyone viewing that station with no regard for individual viewers. Yes, many people might respond to the commercial and the campaign might seem a smashing success. But is it really? What percentage of the many people watching that commercial are in the market for that product?

Divide the broadcast cost by the number of responses and you may discover that the cost per response is very high. This is because the people who respond typically represent a very low percentage of everyone who viewed the commercial. How low? Depending on various factors, the response rate could be 1/10th of one percent or even less. It's like putting drops of food coloring in a bathtub; you won't see any change in the color of the water because the bathtub is very large compared to the few droplets of coloring. In this analogy, the bathtub represents the total viewing population while the food coloring represents the response to that ad.

Say you spend $10,000 marketing to 1,000,000 people and get 1,000 responses, or 1/10%. This ad cost 1 cent per viewer. Not bad, except that you just paid $10 per new customer. Still sound good? That all depends on your net profit per sale. If your product retails for $100, it's entirely possible that you are only making $5-8 after paying all of your expenses (wholesale cost, employees, utilities, rent, etc.). If you just spent $10 to make each sale, then you've just lost $2-5 per sale. Oops. Cheaper product? Double oops.

Enter nanocasting.

What if your product is designed for dogs? Restricting your ads to venues that cater to dog owners shrinks your target audience to about 390,000 people (about

39% of households have dogs). If your product appeals to male dog owners, your target audience is now around 195,000 people (assuming that equal numbers of men and women own dogs). What if your product appeals to male dog owners between 35 and 44 years old? About 8% of people fall into this age range, meaning that your target audience is down to about 15,600 people, or just over 1.5% of the total population of 1,000,000. Your marketing can therefore ignore 984,400 people. In other words, the bathtub is now the size of a Dixie cup. Throw in a few drops of coloring and you'll notice a huge difference.

How huge? Assume that all variables remain equal and that you perfectly target your audience. Your costs shrink from $10,000 to $150 and the same 1,000 people respond to your ad — a 6.4% response rate. Nanocasting drops your cost per customer from $10 to about 15 cents. If your profit was $5 per sale before the ad, then you're clearing $4.85 per sale post-ad. Multiply that by your 1,000 responses and you've just earned $48,500. Beats losing $2,000-5,000, doesn't it?

This example assumes a level of uniformity that is impossible under real world conditions. Does this lessen the impact or importance of nanocasting? Not at all. Play with any number you want (cost of ad, percentage of target audience in the general population, percentage of response, cost per customer) and you'll find that nanocasting beats its bigger cousin in almost every conceivable situation.

Tapping the tremendous power of nanocasting is very easy. Each successive label or qualifier you place on your ideal customer shrinks the number of people you're trying to reach because fewer and fewer people will match all of your specified criteria. However, each drop in overall population increases the percentage of people who will want your specific product. Having identified your target audience, the next step is to find out exactly how to reach them. What specific magazines, newspapers, etc. cater to these people? Combine a highly targeted audience with equally targeted marketing venues, and you're nanocasting. It's that easy.

Nanocasting gives you a much greater bang for your marketing bucks because you'll be spending far less to attract each new customer. Combine this savings with strong follow-up and a solid referral plan and you should start to see some fantastic results for your efforts.

We are not saying that TV and other broadcast media aren't very useful marketing tools, nor are we advocating any one marketing tool over another. Every business is unique and has unique needs. No matter how you market, however, always try to reach the fewest number of people and the highest percentage of people interested in what you have to offer.

WEEK 6
WHAT MAKES YOUR BUSINESS SPECIAL?

One of the first questions we always ask a new client is, "What makes your business special?" More often than not, the reply is a blank look. This is a shame because every business is unique in some way. The differences may not be obvious at first glance but they're always present.

Our definition of flawed marketing is any marketing that is costing too much and/or not having as large an effect as it could have. One of the biggest problems we see with most marketing is that it's all about "me", the business doing the selling, and not about "you", the customer. Combine that with uncertainty about what makes the advertised business unique and you've got the recipe for some seriously flawed marketing efforts. The truth is that customers only care about you to the extent that you satisfy their wants and needs and require a compelling reason to give your business a try.

How do you go about creating customer-focused marketing that shows off how unique your business is?

It's actually quite simple.

Begin by getting out a fresh sheet of paper. On this sheet, list every conceivable benefit customers receive by doing business with you. Don't confuse features with benefits. What's the difference? A feature is a specification or what we call bells and whistles, while a benefit is the end result of said bells and whistles. For example, "250 gigabyte hard drive" is a feature and "holds up to 150,000 songs" (numbers made up) is a benefit. In short, list every last thing your customer can expect to get out of patronizing your business. The key here is to be absolutely brazen and shameless. This is absolutely not the time for modesty!

Your completed list contains all of the reasons why your company is a good one to do business with. We hope it's a long list packed full of meaningful and valuable benefits. Take a few moments to look at this list, both to make sure you haven't forgotten anything and to congratulate yourself on the fabulous job you're doing for your customers. You've worked hard to build the business behind this list and deserve every bit of credit for your efforts.

If your business is alone in its field, then your job is done. Unfortunately, competition is all around you. Your next step must therefore be to research your competition. This may sound like a daunting task and possibly even a depressing one but fear not. Information is power and the more you know about the other players in your field, the better off you'll be.

Researching your competition is a two-step process. First, you need to identify the specific businesses who are competing with you. How? Look around you. Ads, Yellow Pages, the Internet, newspaper ads, direct mail pieces — your competitors are probably doing their level best to make their presence known and should be very easy to find when you go looking for them. If they're not, then either you're looking in the wrong places (bad for you) or your competition may not be doing a good job of marketing (good for you).

Now that you know who the other players in your field are, your next step is to visit each one. This need not be done in person. Look at their ads, marketing collateral, Web sites, etc. What benefits are they advertising? What other unadvertised benefits do they provide to their customers? Compare each competitor benefit to your list. If any competitor offers a benefit that you offer as well, cross it off your list.

What if your competitor lists a benefit that you don't offer? Write it down on a separate list. We'll come back to this in a few moments.

After crossing off all of the benefits that your competitors have in common with your business, sit back and take a look at what's left. Those benefits that have survived the culling are what sets your business apart and what makes you unique. Those benefits are your competitive advantages or what marketers call your USP or Unique Sales Proposition.

Take a long hard look at this list. Are your competitive advantages truly valuable to your customers or are they meaningless fluff? If you can identify at least one of the former, you're OK. If you can identify at least three meaningful competitive advantages, congratulations: Your business is a true standout. If you have more than five solid advantages, you might consider emphasizing different combinations of benefits in different marketing campaigns. We'll talk about that later when we talk about identifying your target audience(s).

Now look at your competition's advantages, those benefits they offer that you don't. For each item on that list, ask yourself the following question: Does my competitor have a serious edge over me, is this benefit just fluff, or is this competitor targeting a different niche of customer? If the former, you need to evaluate your own offerings to mitigate or eliminate your competitor's edge. If any of the latter options apply, don't worry.

The completed list you have in your hand contains your competitive advantages, those unique benefits that you and only you provide to your customers. Memorize this list. Grok it. Live it. Why? Because this is where you're going to hang your marketing hat.

WEEK 7
ENGAGE THE SENSES!

Ponder this: Every piece of information you have about the world reaches your brain through your body's many sensors. This sensory input triggers emotional responses that we validate (rationalize) using our logic. Senses to emotions to logic. That is the human decision-making process.

The marketing implications are clear: Market to the rational mind and you're asking people to synthesize emotions from logic — a backward process with totally unpredictable results. Marketing to the emotional mind puts you on the right track but lacks the raw sensory input. What about marketing to the senses? Do that and you'll trigger powerful emotional responses that people will rationalize into "I need <your product or service> because <reason>."

What do we mean by marketing to the senses? Humans have five means of sensory input: sight, hearing, touch, smell, and taste. Craft your marketing to trigger these senses in the same way that Pavlov used his bell to trigger salivation in his dog. In this example, the dog associated the bell with taste and that delightful sense of relaxed well-being that only a full stomach can provide. Make your marketing the bell that triggers delightful senses in your prospective customers.

Anthony did some work with a small company on the East coast that offers cruises aboard a rustic sailing yacht. He suggested that their marketing tell the story of a short cruise beginning with pulling up to the dock. Talk about the smell of fresh sea salt, the feeling of a refreshing breeze wafting through the hair, the sounds of seagulls and rigging slapping against the mast, the gentle rocking of the boat at night, the taste of hearty meals prepared over the stove. Close your eyes a moment and imagine all this. What emotional response does that trigger in you? Do you feel the call of the open ocean, the freedom from the daily grind, and maybe a bit of pioneering and exploring spirit moving within you? Does this make you more or less likely to want to learn more about this ship?

Don't like ships? No problem. Think about any product or service you use and trace that usage back to your five senses. We don't care if you sell cruises, insurance, real estate, computer repair, tires, food, chotchkes, whatever. There is always a way to tie what you offer into one or more of the five senses. After describing the sensory input, describe the emotions triggered by that input, then rationalize those emotions.

Every business is unique and has certain features and benefits that appeal to different people. We call this the Unique Sales Proposition (USP) or competitive advantages. How can you tie your USP into sensory input and go from there?

Begin by exploring. Put yourself in your customer's position and imagine yourself walking into your business for the first time. What do you see, hear, feel, smell, and taste? Take plenty of time to examine each of the five senses. For sight, look at things such as color, textures, neatness, décor, product arrangement, employee attire, lighting, signs, and layout. For sounds, look at music, ambient noise, sound effects, speech, telephone conversations, product noises, etc. Does your business smell appealing? Depending on your industry, you may not consider smell important, however consider this: What does a bad smell say to you about quality and suitability? Associate a bad smell with just about any business and chances are you won't be in a hurry to return. Do you do business over the phone or via the Internet? How many senses do your customer communications directly access?

Armed with this raw data, how can you emphasize your USP by tying each of your competitive advantages to one or more senses? How can you implant the desire to buy by connecting those evoked senses to specific emotions? How can you have your customers taking the next step of beginning the relationship process with your business by showing them why acting on their emotions is such a good, logical idea? Finally, once you've started this process, how can you keep it going in order to build long-term relationships with your customers?

Figure this out and you may well be on your way to marketing bliss.

WEEK 8
FISSION OR FUSION?

Most businesses are on the lookout for competitors to fight and hopefully defeat. This is a classic example of scarcity-based thinking. People who subscribe to this worldview believe that there isn't enough to go around and that there must be winners and losers. Life is a constant struggle for money, food, power, and status. No matter how much or how little we have, there is never enough because someone named Jones is always one step ahead. We believe this mentality is responsible for the lion's share of human misery.

What if you could turn your marketing swords into plowshares? What if you and your potential competitors could agree that there is plenty of business to go around and come up with a marketing system where everyone benefits? That is abundance-based thinking. People who think abundantly believe that there are enough resources to satisfy everyone's needs and therefore see no need to stay in the rat race. This, dear readers, is the essence of fusion marketing.

Anthony was coming up the stairs from the basement at Allyson's in Ashland, Oregon, when he noticed a series of framed menus from area restaurants hanging on the wall. What a brilliant example of fusion marketing! Yes, those restaurants compete with each other and with Allyson's — at least at first glance.

In a recent chapter, we asked each of you to find out what makes your business special — those benefits you offer that set you apart from the crowd. Armed with that information, it becomes obvious that the restaurants in question may not be quite the competitors common sense might have one believe. Why? Each serves different food. If, for example, Anthony is in the mood for French food, he won't give the Asian place a second glance. If he eats French food tonight, it's a good bet that he'll feel like something different tomorrow, and the Asian restaurant will be that much more attractive. Have dreams of recreating some of the delectable dishes? Allyson's sells the ingredients, the classes, the cookware, and even the wine. Even if two or more restaurants feature the same cuisine, there will still be differences in menu selection, ambience, pricing, location, and more.

Take a good hard look at businesses you feel compete with your own. You should already have done this as part of looking at your competitive advantages. This time, figure out what they offer that you don't. OK, you've probably done this too, most likely to check the robustness of your own offerings. This time, ask yourself how each difference between you and your competitors might appeal to different people.

Why are you doing this? Remember our chapter on nanocasting? Don't try to be all things to all people. Instead, aim to appeal to a very select group of customers. The more selective you are about who your ideal customers are, the less and less of a threat your competitors will pose — and the less of a threat you'll be to them. Just like that, rivals have become neighbors. Can you become friends? Certainly! The next time someone is looking for something that you can't quite match, refer them to one of your neighbors. The customer will appreciate both your thoughtfulness and the pleasure of working with the business that best suits their unique needs. Your neighbor will appreciate the free business. Both the customer and your neighbor will be happy to help you by referring another customer to you. Scratch my back and I'll scratch yours. In marketing, we use the term "fusion marketing partners" to describe businesses who cooperate in this manner.

We used an easy example because food is something we can all identify with.

It isn't always this easy to differentiate yourself and to convince others of the benefits of fusion marketing. That said, we have yet to encounter a situation where fusion marketing can't work.

Also, the example we used only covers businesses in the same industry. Think a clothier, baker, florist, jeweler, caterer, and photographer could form a great fusion marketing alliance? If so, then you've probably been to at least one wedding, costume party, performance, charity event — the list goes on and on.

Nuclear fission is a messy affair that requires both constant monitoring lest it run out of control and someplace to store mountains of extremely toxic by-products. By contrast, nuclear fusion is literally the stuff of stars. We owe our very existence to this elegant process that transforms hydrogen into helium, the stuff of balloons and parties. Fission is about separating and breaking down. Fusion is about coming together. Which example would you like to market by?

Many thanks to Steve and Allyson Holt, owners of Allyson's, for permitting us to mention their business in this chapter.

WEEK 9
YOUR MILEAGE MAY VARY

One day, Anthony was driving back to Ashland from Seattle and continuing a long-running experiment. His car is equipped with a trip computer that displays mileage and distance to empty in real time. Small changes in speed had a huge effect: reducing speed even a few miles per hour increased or decreased his mileage by up to four MPG. Slowing down increased his mileage to a point below which it started dropping again. Hard acceleration also took a big bite out of his distance to empty. Exiting the freeway to do a few minutes of stop-and-go driving in Olympia to visit Amy Levinson? His mileage plummeted. Overall, he averaged over 32MPG; not too shabby for a 255-horsepower V6.

Anthony noticed other things as well. Rolling off the gas as he crested a rise followed by rolling back on as slowly as possible as he reached the bottom and started up the next hill gave him the greatest overall efficiency. The lower speed limits in northern Oregon and Washington meant that one tank of gas lasted the entire 460-mile trip and then some.

What does any of this have to do with marketing?

The keys to Anthony's excellent mileage were pacing, consistency, and subtlety. Let's talk about these three topics in a little more detail.

Pacing. Anthony's normal cruising speed was about 65-70 miles per hour (portions of Washington have the higher speed limit). Slowing to 60 or 55 increased mileage but also increased his trip time. Slowing much below 55 miles per hour would start decreasing his mileage because he'd have to downshift, meaning that the engine would still be spinning as fast while not pushing the wheels as far. Speeding up requires the engine to spin faster, which burns more fuel.

Same with marketing. Getting fast results requires a greater outlay of your resources. Slow down too much and you'll need to spend more to make up for your spotty efforts. Finding your own "sweet spot" for your marketing will give your efforts the best balance of coverage and longevity. Should you advertise weekly or monthly? Should you contact your email list every month or every quarter? Should you focus on TV, radio, word of mouth, or other marketing methods? What combination of marketing methods will give the most mileage for your resources?

Consistency. Freeway driving is much more efficient that stop-and-go city driving. Anthony pulled off the freeway in Olympia for lunch and drove a grand total of perhaps 5 miles before getting back on the interstate. Those 5 miles of inefficient driving cost him several times that many miles of overall range. Stop at a traffic light and you'll expend copious amounts of fuel getting back up to speed. Stop your marketing and you'll need a heavy investment of time, money, and effort to make up for lost time. Remember the old mantra "out of sight, out of mind?"

Never start a marketing campaign that you are unable and/or unwilling to stick with for the long term. You might balk at the ongoing cost and that's perfectly understandable. Trust us when we say that the cost of stop-and-go marketing will be far, far higher in terms of both actual cost and lost effectiveness.

Subtlety. Hard acceleration requires lots of gas. It also tends to discombobulate passengers and cargo alike. Gradual speed changes aren't nearly as sexy (especially when you've got a purring V6 begging for more), but they require far less fuel and don't jar the contents. The students at a marketing training Anthony once presented were coming up with all kinds of suggestions for seasonal marketing campaigns and logo modifications for all the major holidays. Each such change entails costs for a graphic designer, printer, Web master, and more. It also strays from the original marketing message and confuses the target audience who may not necessarily associate the changes with your company.

How about subtle changes that leave the original logo/theme/etc. intact and add a tiny touch? That little dab will give you the seasonal flair you seek while not disturbing your mail message. It will prove far less costly in the long run. Remember, the aim of marketing is not to look fancy or to showcase your artistic talents and whimsy. Your single goal with your marketing is ultimately to increase your profits — something that's rather hard to do if you're not always seeking to extract the most mileage from your efforts.

Market your business as if you were driving a car down the freeway trying to extract every last inch of distance from your limited (and increasingly costly) fuel supply and you will go far. Literally.

WEEK 10
CALLING ALL EXPERTS

What are you an expert in?

Notice that we didn't ask what you do or what your business sells. Do you own a coffee shop? If not, then please pretend that you do for a few minutes. If so, then what you do includes making coffee and tea drinks, possibly some baking, customer service, cleaning, bookkeeping, purchasing, and so forth. If you own a coffee shop, then your business sells coffee, tea, other beverages, baked goods, and the like. And yes, we are stating the obvious.

Most towns have a lot of coffee shops. Competition must exist any time two or more businesses are selling similar or identical products or services in a given area, right?

Yes, if you approach the question from a "what do you do" or "what do you sell" perspective.

Back to the coffee shops. Visit some of the many examples in town and you'll find that the product offerings are where the similarities end. Each shop has its own distinct ambience that appeals to a distinct audience. For example, shop A might find favor with the college crowd while Shop B attracts local artisans. Thus, the owner of Shop A might decide that she is an expert at helping students succeed while Shop B's owner might decide that he is an expert at showcasing local craftspeople.

What just happened? Two businesses with nearly identical product offerings decided that they aren't competitors. A radical idea, yes, but what does it mean?

Since Shop A is the college study expert, they need not bother with the time and expense of marketing in the general media. Instead, they can advertise on campus (if that's allowed), in Laundromats, bookstores, anywhere college students hang out. They could even find other businesses catering to college students as fusion marketing partners. Meanwhile, Shop B can focus on the art scene without bothering to market to the college students.

Both businesses have saved money by nanocasting and have also eliminated the competition by focusing on their expertise instead of their products. Where does the money saved on marketing go? Straight to profits, the dear old bottom line. What is the one measure of business success? Do you see a pattern here? We sure hope so.

We use coffee shops as a random example of a concept that applies to any business. Decide what you are an expert in, then define the exact type of people who need that specific expertise. Your competition will vanish instantly.

So far, we've talked about businesses that sell a narrow range of tightly related products. What if you own a store that sells a wide assortment of different merchandise in different departments? Several examples come to mind in Ashland alone. Does the expertise model apply to you?

Most definitely.

Take a good look at your inventory. What common thread binds all of your products together? Find that thread and you'll be on your way to saying "I am an expert in _____." Now take a look at all businesses who stock some or all of the products you do. What common thread binds them together? We bet it's different than yours for the simple reason that every human being is truly unique and has something original to share with the world. The answer might be readily apparent. If so, congratulations. And if not? Rejoice. Why? Because your expertise will rest in subtle nuances that you can use to fine-tune your marketing even further.

Either way, approaching your marketing from an expertise standpoint is a fantastic way to find the special niche that your business — and only your business — fills in today's crowded business arena. Find that niche that you alone can fill and you'll have far smoother sailing with far fewer competitors. What a beautiful thing.

A few chapters ago, we asked you to determine what makes your business special by listing your benefits and researching your competitive advantages or Unique Sales Proposition (USP). Combine your USP with your equally unique expertise and you'll have one potent marketing message.

WEEK 11
SPEAKING FOR FUN & PROFIT

It is said that the fear of public speaking outweighs the fear of death. Seems some people would rather be the one in the box than the one giving the eulogy. We happen to believe just the opposite and hope you do too because public speaking can be one of your most enjoyable and profitable ways to market your business.

In an earlier chapter, we asked you to find what you're an expert in. Finding your expertise helps you fill a specialized niche and greatly reduce competition.

The road to expertise is paved with credibility. Public speaking is a great way to build credibility. At worst, it costs you nothing. At best, your speaking fees can provide some nice pocket lining.

A solid speech that is both well crafted and well delivered will work miracles. A weak speech that is poorly crafted and/or delivered won't earn you the respect you seek. How does one create a great speech? Easy! Begin with your conclusion. It should be powerful, succinct, and to the point. It should leave your audience thinking "A-ha!" and feeling motivated to take action. Next, what three points best support your desired conclusion and what order should you present them in? Finally, your introduction is the hook that catches people's interest and makes them sit up and pay attention.

New to speaking? It's perfectly OK to use notes. Many speakers at all levels use notes to keep them on track. Not sure what to do with your hands or how to work the stage? Request a lectern or podium. Do you find yourself using words like "and", "um", "so", or others as filler while you search for words? Here's a quick hint: When you feel your words outpacing your thoughts, pause for a few seconds, then continue. This pause helps your last point sink into the audience as you gather your thoughts. It also prevents you from inserting those extra words that risk branding you as an amateur.

Remember that your goal is to build relationships by giving value, not to wheedle money. Make your speech about your audience, never about you. For example, we are rarely if ever the main focus of my chapters except when we describe certain experiences or opinions that relate to the topic at hand.

Where to give your talks? The list is virtually endless. Here are a few ideas tailored to novice speakers: Chambers of Commerce, Elks, Lions, Rotary, Kiwanis, your business, professional organizations, charity events, church events, schools, community centers, convention rooms./centers, public-access TV, local radio (such as Jefferson Public Radio), open mike nights — the list is virtually endless. Which audiences would be most receptive to your talk, and where do they congregate? Nanocasting works here equally well by preventing you from wasting time on audiences who just aren't interested in your particular topic.

OK, so we've given you a few extremely simple pointers. You're raring to go but your fears are holding you back. What can you do? Whatever works. We believe that one's nervousness rises in direct proportion to the importance you place on your words. Nervousness is pent-up energy that you can channel anywhere — such as toward giving a strong, heartfelt presentation. We've each given our fair share of speeches and we are still nervous every time.

Practice, practice, practice. Find a test audience and keep working your message as you develop your unique personal style. Better still, find a test audience whose sole goal is to help you become a great speaker by drawing out and nurturing the skills you already have deep within you.

Where can you find such an organization?

Right in your home town.

Toastmasters International has about 9,000 clubs all around the word with new clubs forming every day. We cannot recommend Toastmasters strongly enough. It's like riding a bicycle where you can fall off as many times as it takes to master the art with nary a scraped knee. Visit www.toastmasters.org to find a club near you and swing on by some time. You'll meet some great people, hear some awesome speeches, and get the chance to add your voice to the human chorus.

Overcoming your fear of public speaking will revolutionize your marketing even if you never give a speech in the traditional sense. You'll even notice that your day-to-day conversations will improve dramatically after joining Toastmasters. Why is this such a good idea for your business? Confident speakers radiate positive energy that uplifts everyone around them. You'll find yourself interacting more effectively with your customers, employees, vendors, and others. You'll network with many people, some of whom will do business with you. You'll develop powerful speeches that will have audience members scrambling for their wallets.

In short, becoming a competent speaker will boost your profits, what Jay affectionately calls the dear old bottom line. And that's what the marketing game is all about!

WEEK 12
YOUR INTELLIGENCE AGENCY

Knowledge is power. In the Information Age, s/he who acquires, processes, and acts on the most information wins. How much information do you have about your business? Does your business have an intelligence agency? If not, you could be in big trouble and not even know it. That's the bad news. The good news is that setting up an effective spying operation is extremely simple, costs next to nothing, and can really grow your profits. Fear not, because this is nowhere near as Orwellian as it might seem. In fact, spying on your own business can be a lot of fun and extremely beneficial.

Why must you do this? You already have lots of information about the mechanics of your business such as vendors, suppliers, product lines, services, employees, consultants, regulations, and finances. You should also have a great deal of information about who your customers are, their likes and dislikes, etc. What else could you possibly need? Plenty.

Remember that marketing is all contact between everyone connected to your business with everyone in the outside world. By "contact", we mean any sensory input obtained using any of the five human senses (sight, sound, smell, touch, and taste). This includes every little detail from how your telephone is answered to employee attire, shop cleanliness, smells — you name it. If someone not in your business senses anything at all about your business, then you are marketing, whether you know it or not.

What impressions are your customers forming about your business thanks to your intentional and unintentional marketing? Are these impressions positive or negative? And why do you need this information?

As a business owner, you are in the relationship business. Keeping happy customers coming back for more and referring their friends and associates is the cheapest and most effective way to grow your profits year over year (see the past chapter on geometric growth). With that in mind, the importance of knowing how you're treating your customers is self-evident.

Getting answers to these all-important questions is simplicity itself. The process consists of two basic steps.

First, spy on your business. Have friends and family members drop in, call, etc. Ask them to make purchases, return items, and ask difficult questions. The key here is that your employees must not know what you're up to and must not know the secret agents involved. You must be able to gather information about your business in its natural state, something that is utterly impossible when people know that you're watching. Your mystery shoppers and callers complete their assignments and report back to you.

Second, tabulate the results. Are you seeing any positive or negative patterns? If the former, keep up the good work. If the latter, then you must take immediate action to correct the problem no matter how trifling it might seem. Believe us when we say that any problems in this area are far, far larger than they appear.

Few customers will voice their complaints because most people avoid confrontation. The vast majority will keep their displeasure to themselves. In fact, only 4% of dissatisfied customers will ever voice a complaint. The other 96% will simply come in and leave with you none the wiser. But that's where the silence ends because every dissatisfied customer will tell 20 people about the lousy experience they had at your business, on average.

Let's put this into perspective. Dissatisfy 100 customers and you'll know about 4 of them. However, 2,000 people will know about you and will be far less inclined to do business with you. Those 2,000 people represent just under 10% of Ashland's population. What percentage do they represent of your home town or neighborhood?

What should you do if you uncover one or more problems? First, don't panic. Second, unless something truly egregious is happening, don't get after your employees. Your problem stems from the unintentional marketing that occurs when one sees marketing as "things to do" such as ads, logos, flyers, etc. The moment you redefine your idea of marketing to include all contact between your business and the outside world, the problem will almost solve itself. Carefully examine every possible means in which customers can come in contact with your business and craft each one to contribute to a positive impression. In most cases, the solutions will be either free or very inexpensive and will normally require very little effort. And the results will be very worth it indeed.

Spying on your business is vital for your success so long as you heed this warning: Conduct a witch-hunt and you will do lasting damage. Conduct a fact-finding mission with the goal of improving our business and you'll have happier customers, happier employees, and a much happier banker!

WEEK 13
YOUR CUSTOMERS AND YOU

The almighty dollar? No such animal. In fact, aside from its use as a universally accepted medium of valuation and exchange, money itself is absolutely meaningless. The customer who chooses where to exchange their money for goods and services is king. Why? Because no one could sell anything without customers. If you are in business then you are 100% dependent on your customers. Period.

In the previous chapter, we talked about the importance of information and emphasized the need to spy on your business as a critical means of proactively finding and addressing customer service problems.

This chapter builds on that by introducing the second component of the customer interaction equation: dialogue.

We have said this before and will keep right on saying it: The #1 problem we see with most marketing is that it's all about "me", the seller, when it should be all about "you," the buyer. Spelling out the unique benefits you offer is the single best approach for finding and retaining customers. Still, it is entirely possible to have a laundry list of benefits and no buyers. Just because you offer it does not mean they will come.

How can you know what your customers want and need? This one is almost too easy.

Ask!

Conducting surveys, asking informal questions, holding customer-appreciation events, and other means of interacting with your customers are all great ways to get inside their heads and find out what they like and dislike about your business.

The most detailed SKU system and barcodes in the world can tell you everything you want to know about what's selling and what's not selling. Subsequent calculations can tell you all about your revenues, costs, and profits by department,

SKU, customer, etc. Based on these numbers, you can get a pretty good idea when it's time to adjust your product lineup. The key words here are "pretty good idea," which is a fancy term for "guess". For all their utility, however, no amount of inventory tracking will tell you what your customers want from you.

Remember that your customers have already taken the hard step of handing over their money to you. They are your best advocates, especially those customers who come back again and again. Like any developing relationship, it won't be long before they will start wishing you carried a certain item or added a certain service. If you don't satisfy their wishes, they may take their business elsewhere. If repeat and referral customers are your lifeblood, customers who stop buying from you are the kiss of death.

Take a few minutes to design a quick survey that should be at once detailed yet require no longer than 5 minutes to complete. Where possible, provide canned answers in a multiple-choice format, being sure to leave enough space for customers to provide additional feedback at will. It's perfectly OK to ask pointed questions as long as they in no way offend the customer or question the wisdom of doing business with you.

So many businesses have comment and suggestion cards that sit quietly gathering dust. How can you be sure your customers see — and act on — yours?

Try training your employees to ask the customer's permission to complete the survey or questionnaire with them at the cash wrap. Alternatively, have someone walking around with a clipboard doing mini-interviews. If your survey includes demographic or other sensitive information (such as income or age), encourage them to fill out your survey and place the completed sheet in an envelope or box to protect their anonymity.

In exchange, offer your customers some incentive for their time, be it a discount coupon, entry in a drawing, or invitation to a special customer-only event. Ask if you can contact them later to continue the dialogue. Above all, make it clear that the purpose behind your questions is to improve their experience with your business.

Products and services are typical survey questions but you need not stop there. You can get all kinds of great information about the entire shopping experience and every single contact your customers make with your business — right down to the smell of fresh bread as they walk past your bakery door (for example). Are these experiences more or less likely to make them return in the future? How can you improve your offerings and the shopping experience?

Take the time to engage your customers in dialogue and solicit their input. Take pains to act on that input and keep improving. Your reward will be happier customers and increased profits. Why? Because while dollars themselves are meaningless, the number of dollars you have and how you wield them will determine the success of your business (or lack thereof).

WEEK 14
CUSTOMER BLISS

Taking customers to a state of bliss is a topic that we are adamant about. Here's a real-life story.

One fine day, Anthony did something completely out of character: he got a straight razor shave. Mike at The Flat Top on Siskiyou Boulevard in Ashland, Oregon, did the honors. To hear Anthony tell it:

"I've probably watched a few too many gangster movies because I was anything but comfortable as Mike leaned the chair back and broke out an instrument whose cousins are responsible for so many celluloid murders. He showed me how the new razors only have 1/32 inch of cutting surface, unlike their older decidedly more machete-like ancestors. Heck, I've gotten worse paper cuts."

"What followed was one of the more relaxing experiences I've enjoyed in a long time. Mike gave me the full treatment — hot towels, layers of warmed shaving cream, a slow unhurried pace, and a face/scalp massage afterward. What began as a fairly stressful experience (yes, I'm squeamish about sharp objects near my throat) left me looking great and feeling refreshed."

How many of us have experienced customer service that feels rushed, impersonal, and/or just plain uncaring? How often have we heard the words, "Have a nice day" as a thinly veiled expression of contempt? In fact, how many of us are so used to interacting with others at arm's length that we've learned to avoid and even shun closer contact?

The act of purchasing is a tremendous leap of faith. Your customer has chosen to invest their hard-earned money on your goods or services. That money represents resources that cannot ever be spent elsewhere. A penny spent, a penny gone. As a business owner or employee, you have a great deal of control over that process. Your customer service can and will make a huge difference in making people feel more or less comfortable about taking that leap of faith.

Here's the best part: Your customers will gladly pay for a wonderful experience. At The Flat Top, the straight razor shave is the most expensive service offered. And you know what? Anthony will do it again.

How does your customer service measure up? The short answer is that you're getting out of it exactly what you're putting into it. A well-known auto muffler and brake chain was converting 70-something percent of phone calls into paying customers. The company added phone training and mandated that only people with that training can answer the phone. Result? They now convert about 96% of their calls into customers.

How many people come into your store on any given day? How many of those make a purchase? How many paying customers are repeat or referral customers? If you're getting good traffic through the door but a disappointing conversion rate, then your customer service needs some rethinking. If you're getting good traffic and good conversion but few repeat or referral customers, then your post-sales follow up needs some work. And if your traffic is less than you'd like? You need to focus on your pre-sales marketing.

Obtaining this information is easy. Set up a system to count people coming in the door. It could be an electronic device or even a person who clicks a counter each time. You can even ask employees to track how many people they contact in a given day and how many customers contact them to see how proactive both employee and customer are about getting together. From there, your register receipt will tell you how many people purchased. Tracking names will give you some insight into how well you're retaining your customers.

If you find a problem? What then? Anthony's three year old son Logan took a dozen eggs and the dishwasher pellets into his room. He unwrapped the pellets and lined them up on a table, then proceeded to drop a few eggs into the glass jar that held the detergent. For good measure, he peeled a couple dozen postage stamps from the office roll and wrapped them around a screwdriver. Anthony was very tempted to get mad and discipline him but soon realized why Logan did it: Anthony was on the phone for a long time unable to pay attention to him. Bored and left to his own devices, Logan decided to do whatever came to mind.

He had absolutely no malicious intent, nor did he try to hide it when Anthony confronted him. Logan did the best he could in the vacuum that Anthony's inattention caused.

Your employees are not children, nor should you treat them like children; however, the parallels remain. Absent your dedication and focused attention on customer service, they will do the best they can with the resources they have. Will it be good enough? In most cases, the answer is no. Not because they're lazy or incompetent. But unless you're directing the customer service effort, there is a higher than average chance that you're letting profit slip between your fingers.

Take your customers to a state of bliss and you will be richly rewarded. Guaranteed.

WEEK 15
RE-SERVE YOUR RIGHTS

No sharing. No refills. No checks. No refunds. No credit cards. Seating limited to 30 minutes. No restroom...

A tremendous assortment of regulatory signs festoons many businesses, some more than others. Our all-time favorite? We reserve the right to refuse service to anyone. Well, of course you have that right. Your business is on private property, is it not?

As a customer, how does it make you feel to walk into a business and be confronted by these kinds of signs and policies? Does reading a sign informing you that the proprietor reserves the right to eighty-six you make you feel more or less welcome and comfortable? Do signs that say "No!" make you more or less likely to linger and shop? Does the sign reminding you that all sales are final make you more or less leery about breaking out your wallet? Our guess is that every such sign, whether it pertains to you personally or not, leaves you feeling a little colder, a little more on edge, a little less relaxed, a little less inclined to purchase. The more customers share this sentiment, the less profitable the business is. Profit is the key measure of business success, meaning that every prospective customer who does not buy reduces the business's success and increases its chance of failure.

As a business owner, you probably put up all of those signs reluctantly and with good reason. After enough people passed dud checks, you decided to avoid the entire problem. Too many people buying stuff to use once and bring back? The occasional undesirable that you don't feel comfortable asking to leave without a sign to back you up? The person who ties up a whole table and plugs their laptop into your power supply to nurse a small coffee all day? These freeloaders were eating away your profit. You had to put a stop to them — and rightly so.

Anthony was chatting about this with his friend and fellow Toastmaster Maia Pepper and she said, "Remember, Anthony, that the word 'reserve' splits into 're serve'." He came home and cracked open a dictionary. Guess what: One of the definitions of "serve" is "To provide goods and services to customers."

Dear readers, today we challenge you to re-serve your rights — in other words, to literally re-focus on providing goods and services to customers.

Problems with bad checks? Add check verification to your credit card terminal. Very cheap and the company will often guarantee the check provided you follow the verification procedure. Don't take credit cards? Get a terminal. Your business will increase by far more than the modest fees charged by the credit card processing companies. Got one of our favorite signs hanging on your wall? Replace it with a new sign that says "We exercise our right to give you excellent service" (and follow that up). Want to discourage people from hogging valuable table space with their computers? Periodically send someone around to ask if they'd like to order something else. Don't accept refunds? Try offering an unconditional money-back guarantee. Some signs, like those silly "No shirt, no shoes, no service" signs might be mandatory. Try adding something like "Oh yeah… pants too!" or some other humorous line to the bottom. In short, replace all of your "No!" signs with "Yes!"

Wait. Won't this result in the same flood of abuse that prompted you to enact those policies and hang those signs in the first place? Not necessarily, provided of course that you take some simple precautions such as check verification, periodic table checks, etc. No, you will probably not be able to stop all of the abuse — but then your current signage isn't achieving that goal, either.

Change "no" into "yes" and add some reasonable precautions and your business will instantly become much more welcoming, a place where the honest majority will feel happier about opening their wallets without even necessarily knowing why on a conscious level. And your profits will probably grow by a large enough percentage to more than make up for the difference.

Here's the secret: You may own your business, but ultimately your customers are the ones who own you. They can get along just fine without you. Can you get along just fine without them? In business, the Golden Rule reads "s/he who has the most gold makes the rules."

Our dear friends, your customers have the gold.

Re-serve your rights!

WEEK 16
MAINTAIN FOCUS

A very large and well-known soda manufacturer once decided that their name means "beverages". So they bought a winery, which tanked — and not in a good way. After this, they decided that their name probably means "soft drinks" and refocused on their core business.

People laugh every time Jay tells this story, but what about your business? What is your focus? Are you making, doing, or selling anything that distracts from that focus? Remember that marketing encompasses all contact between your company and the outside world. It's as if your business is projecting a message. Products and services that deviate from your focus blur the signal. Instead of seeing a crisp clear message, potential customers see a fuzzy picture that makes it harder for them to figure out what you're all about. That lack of clarity makes it harder for them to decide to spend their money at your business. Who loses? You.

For example, one of Anthony's clients was seeking ways to boost her profits. He separated her services into logical divisions and looked at the profits by division. Anthony soon discovered one set of services whose profits were far lower than the others and that required far more resources than the other divisions. She shed the losing services and referred those customers to other companies who specialize in those specific areas. Result? She got more time to provide the services that generate the most profit and netted some fusion marketing partners to boot.

Take a good hard look at your business. How can you organize your products and services into divisions? Having accomplished that, calculate each division's costs, revenue, and profits. If you find any that are performing far below average, consider dropping them and referring those customers to other businesses who specialize in what you're letting go of. See if these other companies will refer business to the parts of your business that you excel at.

How powerful can this be? Say Division A earns $10,000 in profit on $100,000 in earnings. Division B profits $5,000 on $75,000, and Division C profits $15,000 on $125,000. With this example, your business is profiting $30,000 on total revenue of $300,000 — a 10% profit margin. Division B is clearly the losing horse in this race. Dropping Division B and doing nothing else would have your business profiting $25,000 on $225,000 in revenue — a profit margin of 11.1%. Just like that, you've increased your profit margin by 10%. Not too bad for simply letting go.

Freeing yourself from the constraints of losing product and service divisions lets you devote more time and energy into growing the most profitable parts of your business, which can only increase your profits even more. In the above example, were we the business owners, we'd expand Division C to fill the vacuum left by dropping Division B. Doing this would give us more profit and a higher profit margin than we started with. It would also help reduce competition and increase goodwill by referring customers to other businesses.

Money aside, casting off anything that is slowing you down will give you far more time and energy to use any way you wish — possibly even in parts of your life that have nothing to do with your business. How many of us could use more personal time? Jay and Anthony both could.

Find and maintain a laser-like focus on the products and services that produce the most profit with the least cost and you will enjoy higher profits, more time and energy, fewer hassles, and a lot less stress.

WEEK 17
SHOPPING FOR PROFITS

Imagine running pell-mell down supermarket aisles blindfolded, tossing random ingredients into your shopping cart. Our guess is that you'll end up with a few ingredients that you'll use, more that you'll try and dislike, and a solid majority that you will never use. Now imagine taking a few moments to plan your menu before going shopping. Our guess is that you'll put all of your selected ingredients to good use.

How does this relate to marketing?

Think of every possible way to market a business (direct mail, newspaper ad, business card, etc.) as an ingredient. Do you consider marketing to be a series of actions or events? If so, then you are approaching your marketing from a "things to do" perspective. You may have lots of marketing out there, but what is the plan behind those efforts? Marketing without a plan is like running blindfolded through supermarket aisles as described above.

Here's an example: You decide that you need a brochure, newspaper ad, direct mail campaign, Web site, business cards, and coupons. Great! So how do you plan to use them? What is your process for reaching out to prospective customers and guiding them through the soft steps to ease the stress of purchasing from you? Without a plan, you have no way to know and are therefore risking spending way too much on marketing that will return way too little. Failure to plan is one of the biggest problems we see with most marketing.

On the other hand, if you devise a marketing plan with very specific goals and tailor each marketing action to that plan, then you will be like the second shopper who created a shopping list prior to setting out. We think most people would agree that the best way to shop for groceries is to work your way backward from "What do I want to eat?" to "What ingredients do I need?" to "What do I have in stock?" to "What else do I need?" Same with your marketing.

Try this simple exercise: Ask yourself, "What specific result do I want to achieve?" followed by, "What specific process should I use to achieve my desired results?" followed by, "What marketing method best suits each step of this process?" Work your way backward and your profits will work their way upward.

To continue the previous example, you might decide that your newspaper ad should direct people to your Web site. This site contains complete details about your products and services, any options such as color and size, and directions to the store. It also offers a free newsletter or other giveaway. Customers who arrive at your store will usually know exactly what they're looking for, making the purchase fast and easy and letting your staff help far more customers than before. Each customer gets a business card from their personal representative who they may contact at any time with questions or problems. If they mention your Web site, they get a coupon for 20% off their initial purchase. After the sale, they receive a brochure thanking them for their business, reiterating your 100% guarantee, and asking them to refer other customers to you. And the direct mail piece? You may find that it's more expensive than all of the other marketing methods combined and drop it. Or not.

Keep in mind that your desired end result might not be to simply drive traffic into your store. You might advertise a sale on men's shirts — a different undertaking than doing the same thing for women's shirts. Your goal could be as simple as getting people onto your email list where they can receive value-packed information that will both help them and keep your business in their minds. The possibilities are endless. The key is to be as specific as possible.

Notice that we're not discussing the quality of the ingredients. The freshest kiwi fruit in the world won't appeal to Anthony's wife. The best-looking brochures, Web sites, etc. in the world won't deliver their maximum possible impact without a plan. Here again, it's not the ingredients.

Think about your marketing. Has it revolved around solid plans? If so, congratulations! And if not? That's OK too. No matter what, the fact that you're in business at all means that you're doing a lot of things right. Focus on each of the many things you do right every day and take a few moments to savor those accomplishments. Come from that happy place when planning your improvements and you'll have both lots of fun during the process and lots of profits afterward.

WEEK 18
CULTIVATING ELEGANCE

The dictionary defines "elegance" as "refinement, grace, and beauty in movement, appearance, or manners." Watch a true professional at work, be it washing windows, digging ditches, gardening, building, you name it. Contrast that with an amateur doing the same thing. For example, a professional window washer wields a squeegee with sinuous movements that achieve far cleaner results in far less time than most of us can ever hope for. There is nothing menial about that or anyone who has elevated their profession (however humble it might seem) to a state of elegance, for that is art. How can you elevate your business to an art form?

Far too many clients of ours have been struggling to expand their profits and working ever-longer days in that quest. One landscaping company provides a wonderful case in point: The owner has reams of data and analysis and has been banging her head against walls trying to think her way through. The good news is that she recently discovered how to roughly triple her profit with no additional effort. The problem is that further growth will require either more hours (not good for the soul) or hiring additional help (and there go the newly found profits). One of the things she misses most is enjoying her art (watercolor, dance, and singing). By thinking her way through, she was stifling her creativity and sinking deeper into the struggle of growing her business.

Does any of this sound familiar to you? If so, we have a few questions: What if nothing is sacred? What if the mere fact that your business has certain processes and certain ways of doing them means nothing? What if you could dance, paint, sing, or sculpt your way to ease and joy?

We invite you to forget everything you know about running your business. Pretend you're back at the beginning, those heady days when ideas flowed like water and the excitement was electric. Let those wonderful feelings surround and permeate you. Then build your ideal business, only don't do it with business plans and calculators. Instead, express your vision through your art.

If you're a painter, paint your ideal business complete with every step of every process. If you're a musician, compose a piece that does the same thing. Sculptor? Actor? Author? Mime? Same idea. This isn't about painting diagrams, sculpting floor plans, or committing your employee handbook to song (unless you want to). Rather, the goal is to create artistic representations that may bear no logical resemblance to what they describe. And that's OK; the idea is to stop thinking and allow your creativity to do what it does naturally: create.

Because you're creating an expression of your perfect business, your subconscious mind will be going over every last little aspect of that ideal vision while your conscious mind is creating something that may seem totally unrelated. You'll start coming up with lots of ideas about what is and is not essential to your business and ways to make each essential piece as elegant as possible. The process of creating art is the process of creating elegance. That elegance is what draws people to museums, theaters, concerts, and more. It is what will draw you toward realizing your ideal business.

The landscaping lady now reserves one hour each day for personal time. She lamented the prospect of budgeting even more time to squeeze in her art. Imagine her delight upon learning that her personal hour can also be her time for artistic expression and that freeing her creativity would benefit both herself and her business.

Just like that she gained an hour filled with abundant joy, fulfillment, and productivity. One can only imagine the bounty to come.

Elegance: refinement, grace, and beauty in movement, appearance, or manners. What elegance will your inner artist create for your business?

Give it a try. The results will amaze you.

WEEK 19
WHAT'S YOUR PROCESS?

What is your marketing process? What measurable, clearly defined steps do you take to convert a lead into a prospect, a prospect into a customer, and a customer into a lifelong client? If you've been following these chapters, you know that marketing is a courtship ritual that encompasses all contact between anyone in your business with everyone outside it. So what's your ritual?

Imagine you are sitting somewhere minding your own business. A total stranger approaches and asks whether you'd care to find a room and get friendly. Our guess is that the odds of your saying yes are pretty low. On the off chance you do accept the offer, the odds of your partner ever contacting you again are… well… minimal.

Question: Does this sound like most marketing you see every day that wants you to make the purchase and then vanish? Does it remind you of your own marketing efforts? We call this approach Friday night marketing. Friday night marketing relies on spreading a message far and wide in hopes (literally) of getting lucky. Sure, these ads might be targeted (you are, after all, far more likely to be approached in a singles bar than at your local eatery) but their approach and tone remain the same: buy, buy today, and happy trails.

Let's return to our example, only this time the stranger asks if you'd like to go for coffee. Are the odds of your saying yes to coffee higher or lower than the odds of your accepting the more personal offer? My guess is those odds are far higher. You go to coffee and have a wonderful time with no pressure whatsoever. Afterwards, your new acquaintance invites you to lunch, another very easy step to take. From there, things progress to dinner, walks on the beach, and more until one day this former stranger asks for your hand in marriage. By this time, that huge step, that ultimate leap of relationship faith, has been rendered far easier by the step-by-step courtship ritual. And after the marriage? In theory, you and your partner remain together forever. Their family and friends become yours and vice-versa. In other words, the marriage connects each of you to each other's networks.

The trick here is twofold: One is to craft a process that consists of a series of well-defined and measurable steps towards a sale and then taps into your customers' networks post-sale. Two is to design your marketing so that each step only asks prospects to take the next step.

Why is having a clearly defined process a good idea? You might know that you're converting, say, 12% of your prospects into customers. But where are you losing the other 88%? Without a clearly defined process, you might have no idea what you're doing right and where you're going wrong. Change your existing methods and you risk breaking the one thing that's working for you. On the other hand, if you have a clearly defined series of steps, you could easily see that you're losing 65% of your prospects at Step 5. Fix Step 5 (and Step 5 only), and your conversion rate will skyrocket. Best of all, this change should require very little time and effort because you know exactly what needs fixing and can zero in on the problem without breaking what wasn't broken.

Why does each step of the process only ask customers to take the next step? For the same reason you only ask someone you're interested in out to something easy like coffee: This step-by-step progression builds the foundation for lasting trust, rapport, and business.

How much business? Imagine you're selling a $100 product that the average person buys 3 times per year for 20 years. Use Friday night marketing and you'll pocket your $100. Create a process to ease prospects into becoming customers and then keeps them and their friends coming back for more and the numbers jump. Say each customer refers 3 friends who all follow the average purchasing pattern. This $100 sale has just become $24,000 ($100 x 3 sales per year x 20 years x 4 people). Which would you prefer?

Relationship marketing using well-defined processes takes time, just like it takes time for a seedling to bear fruit. You'll need to invest lots of water, fertilizer, and love before you can reap the benefits of your labor. The results, however, can be very well worth it — especially if you take advantage of the most potent marketing tool there is, a tool that can only work with relationship marketing.

WEEK 20
SELLING WITHOUT SELLING

Would you like us to reveal the most powerful marketing tool there is (at least in our expert opinions)? Good, because here goes…

We are surrounded by marketing, to the tune of several thousand messages per day. Marketing has become so pervasive that we don't even consciously register it anymore except in special cases. Do they register subconsciously? Probably, but do you, as a small business, have the resources it takes to bombard your audience so thoroughly that they have no choice but to remember you?

Of course not. This leaves you with a choice. You could decide to add your message to the blizzard and get lost in the marketing storm — a time — and money-burning machine. Or you could simply decide to opt out and step away from the maelstrom because you might just be able to sell far more without selling at all.

Selling without selling is far easier and much more cost-effective than it first sounds. All you need to do is to abandon the taking stance and slip into a giving stance. Instead of asking what your prospects and customers can do for you, ask yourself what you can do for them.

For example, the owners of a new restaurant Jay knows about discovered that most of their clientele frequent salons. What did they do? They visited every salon within a 1- to 2-mile radius and offered the owners a free dinner for two. Not one of those "buy one, get one of equal or lesser value" coupons, but a totally complimentary meal with drinks, dessert, anything they wanted, as much as they wanted, with no strings attached. Result? Business boomed. Why? Because the salon owners had a wonderful experience and were never pressured or even asked to buy anything. This combined with the gift of a delicious meal made them evangelists. Can't you almost see them gabbing up the new restaurant with every one of their clients and the clients getting hungrier and hungrier as they sit there thinking about the possibilities?

Question: How much less did this campaign cost and how much more effective was it than going the traditional advertising route? Jay doesn't have exact figures but our guess to both questions is "lots". Instead of using brute advertising dollars, this restaurant invested in relationships, soft steps, and giving to the community. And the community responded.

There is one major caveat: When you're giving something, always make the gift about the receiver. How would you react if someone gave you a coupon for a free dinner only to follow that up with "We've just opened a new restaurant and are out recruiting affiliates to send diners our way?" Probably not too favorably. Now what if this person gave you the coupon saying something like "We've just opened a new restaurant and would be honored to invite you and a friend to be our guest for dinner." See the subtle difference? By not trying to sell anything, the chances of making a sale have just risen dramatically in this example.

What about you? What can you give? Actions in the form of actual products and services speak far louder than any ad copy. How can you give? There are lots of ways. You can give free demonstrations, free samples, free products or services, free information, free consultations, charity work, sponsor a Little League team — the list goes on and on.

Remember that you need not give away the store. In fact, excessive giving is a fast track to lowered profits. Further, you need not necessarily give to everyone. In the restaurant's case, they gave to salon owners. If you have this clear an audience, give to them. If your audience is more general, find a way to give something small and valuable that everyone can use. Those people who express interest get a larger sample.

Here's an example that most of you are familiar with by now: Offering everyone a free coaching/consulting session would quickly overwhelm Jay or Anthony. Giving everyone a newspaper column or free online newsletter that reaches thousands of people is very easy to do. Those people who are interested can then take advantage of the free coaching session. Everyone gets something and we invest the majority of our resources on the people who are the most interested. A win-win. Please note that we mention our examples merely because they are real-world examples of what we're talking about, not because we're trying to break our own rules.

Adopt a giving stance and build that into your soft-step marketing structure and you'll spend far less on marketing and will reap far greater rewards because you'll be stepping out of the Babel of incessant ads that are trying to get something out of you.

WEEK 21
WHO'S STEERING THE SHIP?

So Jay gets a call from a new client who wants some help managing his time better. The client is so swamped that he can't keep the initial phone meeting and, when they finally connect, keeps interrupting to put out fires. After we finished chuckling at the irony, we realized that similar problems plague many if not most business owners.

Imagine a ship.

The captain stands on the bridge directing the ship's course and speed and ensuring that its mission gets carried out. The first mate handles most of the administrative management, which includes much of the paperwork. Below them, the department heads handle their specific areas of the ship. The Engineering Officer manages the engines, generators, and other machinery while the Deck Officer manages things like lines and painting. Other officers handle their own individual areas of responsibility.

The captain never bothers with shoveling coal, changing oil, chipping paint, handling mooring lines, etc. Her or his job is to see the ship safely from port to port and to be the final overseer of onboard operations. Period. The Engineering Officer never worries about chipping paint. You get the idea. Everyone has a function that serves the greater good and sticks to that function as much as possible.

How many of you are trying to steer the ship and shovel coal at the same time? How many of you want to grow your businesses but dread the extra hours of effort such expansion would entail?

The solution is simple: As the owner, you are the captain of your business. If you're a one-person show, you must indeed do everything yourself. But if you have partners and/or employees? At this point, careful delegation becomes a key requirement for growth.

How do you spend your time? There are four basic types of tasks:

- Important and not urgent. Tasks in this category will have long-lasting implications for your business but don't need to be handled right away. This is where you should be spending about 50% of your time.

- Important and urgent. These are the true emergencies that can impact your business and must be addressed post haste. Under ideal circumstances, things in this category will only happen rarely, if at all. Good time management and effective systems go a long way to keeping these occurrences to a minimum.

- Not important and urgent. This category is usually what people are referring to when they speak of "putting out fires". Think about the many fires you've extinguished in your career. In hindsight, how many of these incidents had real potential to impact your business? Probably not many. Here again, good systems go a long way to mitigating this category. If you have employees or partners, delegation can be especially powerful here because people can manage things in their own areas, often without having to bother you.

- Not important and not urgent. If something will have no impact on your business and need not be addressed any time soon, just how much of your time and energy does it require?

Focus on guiding your company forward, on making the decisions that will have positive impacts on your business and your life. Delegate as much as possible of the rest to the appropriate people. We're not saying you need to abandon your responsibilities or simply dump work on others. We are saying that your ship needs you on the bridge and someone else minding the engines.

Start by getting out a sheet of paper and listing every single function your company performs. It may surprise you how little of what you do involves your company's specialty. For example, if you own a bakery, the actual baking comprises only a tiny fraction of the many things your company must do to survive and thrive. In fact, the baking itself is probably little more than an afterthought!

Armed with this list, your next step is to look at your people and decide who can best handle each item. Once you've done this, start handing off the chosen tasks to your chosen people. Do this and you'll find yourself with a lot more time and energy on your hands, time that you can use to focus on growing your business. You may have to pay your people more to take on the added responsibilities, but the freedom you buy with that money will pay for itself many times over provided you invest that freedom wisely.

WEEK 22
OWNER BLISS

Does your business serve you or are you serving your business?

Finding that answer is as easy as answering the following question: When is the last time you did something that was totally and completely all about being good to and pampering yourself? If the exact particulars of date, time, activity, and people involved have not already sprung to mind as you read this, then it's been way too long.

Do you fit into this category? If so, did you go into business expecting freedom from the restraints of a traditional job only to find yourself trapped by the many demands of owning and operating your own concern? By now, you've probably discovered that your product or service is almost an afterthought compared to the many tasks and processes required to keep a business up and running. Far too many entrepreneurs fall into the trap of being slaves to the businesses that should be serving their wants and needs. This leads to burnout, a variety of attempts to cope, and possibly even failure.

A long time ago, we learned a very simple lesson: No one on this planet is so important that the world can't get by just fine without them for a little while. Same goes for your business. Whether you believe it or not, you can step away for a little while and things will keep humming merrily along. So what are you waiting for?

As soon as possible (certainly within the next two weeks), we urge you to leave your business and do something to pamper yourself. It could be as easy as going for a hike or watching a sunset. It could be as involved as getting a complete spa treatment or a night on the town. You decide. The only criteria you need to meet is that whatever you do must be completely and totally about you and no one else.

Try to relax fully into the experience once it occurs instead of worrying about the many things that might (but probably aren't) going wrong in your absence. Do that and you'll emerge with your batteries recharged and ready to go back to work. The trick is to do this as regularly as possible to keep your stress level down and to create a strong mental association between your business and being good to yourself. You created this business. Shouldn't it be good to and for you?

What does any of this have to do with marketing?

One word: Energy

A stressed-out boss spreads that stress to her or his employees and creates a tense vibe that permeates the entire business. Customers experience this vibe the moment they walk in the door and get a double dose when they encounter your employees and receive curt and/or inattentive treatment. Anthony once stepped into a restaurant where it was clear the owners had been arguing only moments before. The tension was so thick as he ate that he never returned. Did the owners' stress levels affect their bottom line? You bet.

If time management is your issue, my previous chapter has some quick tips to help you start getting a handle on your time and there are plenty of great resources out there. If you're worried that less time in your business means less profits, we know at least one person who is on track to triple her profits while cutting 15 hours per week off her schedule.

If cash flow is your issue, there are many things you may be able to do to boost your profits immediately. We'll talk about pricing later. Beyond pricing, you may be able to reduce expenditures in various ways by increasing efficiency and/or closing down unprofitable parts of your business.

If a strong sense of duty is your issue, well, yes, you must give your business the attention it deserves. The flip side of that is that your business can only be as healthy and vibrant as you are. If there is something wrong with your business, the mirror is usually a good place to start looking. Never forget that your prime duty and responsibility is to yourself for without yourself, you have and are nothing at all.

Be good to yourself and your business will be good to you. Just as importantly, it will be good to your customers, who will be far more likely to visit you again in the future.

So how are you going to pamper yourself this week?

WEEK 23
PREPARING FOR GROWTH

What if your business doubled — and we do mean doubled — overnight? Sure, you'd have twice your sales and twice your profits. You'd also have double your employees, customers, locations, vendors, etc.

The simple truth is that your actual product or service is almost an afterthought compared to the many tasks and systems required to run a business. Many people start businesses because they enjoy making the product or providing the service and end up putting in longer and longer days and falling further and further behind. It's what Michael Gerber calls "working in your business instead of on your business." How can you regain control of your time and start moving forward instead of treading water?

It's very easy.

Begin by examining every process and function in your business and eliminate anything that is not essential. Be as objective as possible. You may just find yourself spending a significant amount of time on insignificant tasks. Lose those and you'll recapture both time and energy.

Divide the essential items into strategic and tactical.

Strategic items affect the direction and focus of your business in general and include marketing, planning, networking, etc. Tactical items affect portions of your business, such as payroll, accounts payable, inventory, estimating, etc. As the owner, you must focus on the strategic items just like the captain of a ship focuses on getting the ship where it needs to be. Decide who in your business can best handle the tactical items and delegate them accordingly.

Eliminate your non-essential tasks and functions and properly delegate the rest and you may well surprise yourself with the many hours you save each week.

So how will you use all the time you gain?

One idea might be to tackle any long-term goals you may have been putting off. One method of doing this that we've seen work uses the following four steps:

- First, break the goal down into simple steps that you can accomplish on a weekly basis.

- Second, forget about the goal and focus solely on the step you're currently taking. The step you took last week is over and no longer matters. The step you'll take next hasn't arrived yet and does not yet matter to you.

- Third, do each step as it comes up. If you find yourself hitting a wall, simply divide each step in two and slow down. If you find yourself inspired to move faster, double up your steps each week. Accelerate or decelerate as needed. Just keep moving forward no matter what.

- The fourth and final step is in many ways the most critical. Before undertaking each step, decide how you will reward yourself for accomplishing it. This reward need not be expensive nor time-consuming. It must, however, be both creative and meaningful. For example, if you go out to dinner frequently, don't reward yourself by going out to dinner. Read a book, see a sunset, go for a hike — what you do is not important. What is important is that you program yourself to associate joy and taking care of yourself with accomplishing the things that really matter to you.

People have shared that they've shaved as much as 15 to 25 hours from their weekly schedules. We can't guarantee how much time you'll manage to save each week. That said, every minute saved is a minute gained. How will you use it?

Imagine that you've eliminated needless tasks, categorized and delegated your essential tasks, and are making measurable progress toward your long-term goals. Now how does the prospect of doubling your business sound?

Maybe you don't want to double your business. Maybe you want to have more time for family, friends, volunteer organizations, a second enterprise, traveling, or pampering yourself. It's up to you because it's your time. If there is one thing that unites all of us, it's that none of us has forever.

WEEK 24
THE BEST FOUR-LETTER WORD EVER

We tend to look down on four-letter words, often with good reason. Today, however, Jay would like to introduce you to the best four-letter word you'll ever see for your business:

Free.

This small word has the potential to completely transform your marketing. Look at it this way: You probably already invest time and money proclaiming how wonderful your business is. What if you could invest a portion of those resources in proving it? Talk is cheap. Action is everything.

What can you offer for free to establish yourself with prospective customers and/or stay in touch with existing customers? The list is nearly infinite. Here are some ideas to spur your creativity:

- **Free consultations:** No matter what business you're in, chances are there are lots of similar establishments hawking their own wares. What if you advertised not your products or services but a free consultation on how to select the best of what's available? Anthony suggested to his housekeeper that she offer a free 15-minute consultation in her classified ad. She tried it and has been buried under prospective customers ever since. Same for the chiropractor Jay worked with.

- **Free gifts:** A major bank sent out a mailing advertising financial services to high-net-worth prospects. Some mailings contained an offer for a free leatherette notebook that cost somewhere under $2 apiece while others did not. The mailings with the free offer outperformed their cousins by a factor of about 4 to 1. What's interesting is the very low cost of the gift relative to the target audience. This proves that your free gifts need not be extravagant. Don't hand out junk, just don't spend a fortune.

> • Free samples. Free upgrades. Free newsletters. Free products. As we said, the list goes on and on and on.

Why is this such a potent marketing tool? Two reasons.

First, the typical ad makes some big claims and asks for the sale. What does this tell you, the potential customer, about the quality of the business and its goods and services? Nothing, but it does tell you that they want your money, all too often in no uncertain terms. Offering something for free gives the customer the chance to try you out in a totally risk-free environment. Once they've gotten a taste of the wonderful quality and superlative service you offer, they'll be far more inclined to come back for more.

Second, remember that the best way to sell is by not selling at all. Adopting a giving versus a taking stance will yield far more results in the long term. Case in point: A jewelry store in Medford, Oregon, once offered an evening of free pizza and sports on a big-screen TV. Attendees received a consultation on how to select jewelry for their significant others. That idea struck both of us as one of the most brilliant ideas we've ever seen and we're dying of curiosity to learn how it worked.

So far we have been talking about prospective customers. What about existing customers?

Jay is going to let you in on a little secret: Finding ways to give free things to your existing customers may well be the single most amazing marketing tool you'll ever employ. Think about this: Your existing customers have already taken the hard step of giving you their hard-earned money, thereby demonstrating the ultimate act of commercial faith. If they did it once, there is an excellent chance that they will do so repeatedly. You can enhance this chance by showing them that their relationship with you is a two-way street.

If you sell auto parts or service, try offering free car washes for a year. Finding a car wash place that would gladly discount their prices in exchange for the free business should be fairly easy. Think they might be willing to tell their customers about you, thus giving you a fusion marketing partnership? We do too.

Do you sell personal services (especially that have to do with having fun and/or taking care of one's self)? How about a "bring a friend free" offer? This could also work well for some of the more seasonal businesses during the slow period. You're paying your fixed costs no matter what, so why not take the chance to introduce new people to your business?

Your ability to offer free goods and services to your existing customers does of course mean that you need to know who these people are and have some sort of process for following up with them to keep the relationship alive. That, dear readers, is the topic of next week's chapter.

These few examples in this chapter randomly sprang to mind as we typed. As an entrepreneur, you are creative and imaginative by nature. Use that creativity to come up with innovative offers for your prospective and existing customers and you may find yourself reaping the rewards of increased profits.

WEEK 25
TAPPING THE EXISTING CUSTOMER WELL

In the last chapter, we talked about the power of the word "free" and suggested that offering freebies to your existing customers might well be your single best marketing tool. This brings up a bigger question:

What process do you have for following up with and retaining your existing customers?

Here's the stark truth: If you are not already rattling off your step-by-step follow-up process, then you are walking away from some of the easiest profit you'll ever make. Period.

Your prospective customers must grapple with the decision whether or not to spend some of their money in your business. We have said it before and we'll keep saying it: The act of handing over money is the ultimate act of consumer faith. By contrast, your existing customers have already taken the plunge. If you've done your part right, they found that an enjoyable and satisfying experience.

Existing customers have two major advantages over prospective customers: First, they'll tell all their friends about their purchase — particularly if it was major or otherwise significant. Second, they'll be far more likely to buy from you again. Tapping your well of existing customers is the easiest, cheapest, and most profitable thing you'll ever do for your business. Sadly, far too many businesses miss this golden opportunity. The customer's initial excitement fades and they become once again susceptible to the thousands of marketing messages your competitors and other businesses bombard them with every single day. Your customer has a limited supply of dollars. You've already made the effort to sell them on your products and services. Why let all that go to waste?

How do you keep existing customers coming back for more? This is almost too easy in most cases. First, make the buying experience as pleasant as possible.

Customers who associate good feelings with your business are far more likely to return. Second, remember that existing customers are not prospects. Don't market to them in the same way that you market to new customers. Third, remember that the period of maximum satisfaction extends for 30 days from the purchase date. Beyond that and your great product or service will become just one more thing in your customer's home or business. Keep these three things in mind and your customer follow-up plan will be off to a great start.

What tools can you use in your follow-up plan? There is a vast list of possibilities. How about a frequent purchase card? A customer-only club where you offer special deals? Bring a friend free? Little extra gifts you throw in the bag as a thank-you for the repeat business? Freebies and discounts for referring others? If you know exactly what they bought (you do track each customer and their purchases, don't you?), how about recommending other purchases? For example, if Mrs. Jones bought a certain shirt, you could offer matching accessories. How about a free email newsletter with tips on how to use and maintain their purchases? A guestbook? Mailing a sample of new products?

Easiest of all, how about a simple phone call 30 days after the sale asking how the customer likes their purchase and if they have any questions? Mrs. Jones, you purchased the silk blouse on the second. How are you enjoying your new outfit? I remember how great you looked when you tried it on. How does it fit? Do you have any questions? By the way, I just got in some slacks that would look fabulous with that top. This may sound cheesy but the results can be spectacular — especially if you ask for their contact information and tell them that you always follow up with customers 30 days later to make sure they're absolutely happy.

So far we've talked about products. How about services? Maybe you offer spa treatments. How about snapping a photo of your customer when she walks in followed by another immediately upon completing your treatment? Get a photo printer and create a postcard with the before and after pictures side-by-side. Mail it to your customer with an offer for her next visit. Anthony once worked with a sailing cruise company. He suggested that they snap candid photos of guests enjoying themselves on deck and mail it to them after the cruise in a beautiful frame — with the company logo discreetly but definitely present.

Devise a step-by-step process for retaining your existing customers by following up with them. This process must be repeatable and tailored specifically to existing customers in addition to following all of your other marketing rules. This will require some time and innovation on your part but the returns will be extremely well worth it. Guaranteed.

Speaking of guarantees, that's the topic for next week's chapter. Stay tuned.

WEEK 26
GUARANTEE INCREASED SUCCESS

What kind of guarantee do you offer on the products and/or services that you sell?

Many businesses have fairly restrictive refund policies and limited to no guarantees. A very sensible approach. After all, who wants to be saddled with returns caused by everything ranging from defects to wishy-washy customers? The paperwork alone is a nightmare let alone trying to wrangle credits from vendors because the whole commercial engine is geared towards driving products to consumers, not away from them. Increase your guarantee and your returns will skyrocket along with the numerous headaches they bring.

This logic is perfectly sound.

Paradoxically, however, the reverse is true: The more liberal the guarantee, the fewer returns come in. Yes, you read that correctly: Increase your guarantee and your rate of returns will decrease. Pretend you walk into Store A and see an item with a 30-day guarantee. Store B carries the exact same item and offers a 1-year guarantee. Store C offers a lifetime guarantee: If the thing ever breaks or becomes otherwise unusable, bring it back for replacement or refund.

Assuming all else is equal about the product, which store would you purchase from? We would be very surprised if you said anything but "Store C". But why?

Think about the subtle, almost subconscious implications behind the 30-day guarantee. It literally tells you that you'd best figure out pretty darn quickly whether you made the right decision or not. It also makes you wonder if your purchase will last much beyond Day 31. Do you get our point? The restrictive policy sends the clear message that you don't have faith in your own products, or that your faith is only good to a limited point. That message makes customers wary to make the purchase in the first place and more apt to return the product later. If you offer a 30-day guarantee, expect to see lots of returns by around Day 28 or so. The 1-year warranty is much better. However, it too sends the same message, albeit not as strongly as its 30-day cousin.

And the unlimited guarantee? Think about it a moment. The seller is so confident in his products that he is perfectly happy to stand behind them 100%. Confidence is contagious. We all like confident people. We want to know that the people we spend our increasingly hard-earned dollars on will be there when we need them. When do we need them? When things go wrong.

Whether you offer products or services and no matter how you offer them (retail location, online, in person, etc.), there is one question we'd like you to ponder: What can you do to transfer the risk of purchasing from your customers' shoulders to your own? Caveat emptor (buyer beware) may have worked in past centuries but it won't work in the new millennium. We'll say it yet again: Making a purchase, actually forking over money, is the ultimate act of commercial faith. Thus, our question stands: How can you make that decision as risk-free as possible? Answer: A strong guarantee. Find a way, any way, to relieve your customer of as much risk as possible.

Costco has one of the most liberal return policies we know. If something breaks or if you just don't like it, take it back and you'll receive full credit. We both love Costco and have purchased our share of big-ticket items from them because we know that they stand behind what they sell. They can do this because they sell truly excellent stuff. How can you emulate that model?

Join Jay's Guerrilla Marketing Association and you'll get both a free month of membership plus the ability to opt out at any time with never any pressure whatsoever. The Guerrilla Marketing Association boasts a growing cadre of longtime members, each of whom is receiving valuable tools for growing her or his business.

Anthony offers all new clients an initial coaching/consulting session. If they opt to continue using his services, he offers three more sessions. Then and only then does he bill for those four sessions, provided that the client is delighted with his services. If they are not delighted, he discontinues the relationship and they owe him nothing. Going forward, Anthony bills at the end of every month of service. In this way, the risk is always where it belongs — on the seller's shoulders. Anthony's return (non-payment) rate among people who go the month is zero. Can you do something similar in your own business?

Yes, there are some things you can't and shouldn't take back, and we're sure you can think of examples without our having to go into detail. Yes, there is also the potential for abuse. The good news is that diligently tracking your sales can reduce any abuse to a very low level. You do track your sales, don't you? If not, there are lots of reasons why you should. We'll get to that in a future chapter.

Find ways to reduce the risk to your customers and your profits will increase. We guarantee it.

WEEK 27
PRICING 101

We've worked with our fair share of clients and pricing is a perennial issue. More entrepreneurs than we'd care to count seem to think that business will roll in if they can only lower their prices far enough. They slash and burn like rainforest farmers gone amok and wonder why customers aren't streaming in.

The answer is very simple: Price is far less important than value. Think about your own purchasing behavior. Just how often do you go out of your way to scrimp a few pennies? How often do you spring for the "el cheapo" model of anything? By now you probably know that shortcuts make for long delays. The few pennies you save by schlepping to the low price leader are often more than equaled in time, gas, and hassle. The el cheapo model breaks at the worst possible moment leaving you inconvenienced at best and kicking yourself for your penny wise, pound foolish ways.

Human beings are astoundingly consistent creatures and what holds true for you also holds true for your customers. The bottom line is that only 14% or so of customers cite price as their primary buying criterion. The good news is that you can probably charge far more than 14% thanks to the "you get what you pay for" rule. In short, never compete on price. Well, almost never.

Where should you price your products or services? Here's a good rule of thumb: Find the high and low prices for similar offerings in you area, then set your price at the 80th percentile. For example, if the lowest price is $100 and the highest is $200, price yourself at $180. If nothing else, this is an excellent starting point because it keeps you well clear of the pricing trap by allowing you to compete on value instead of on price. This is a very good thing.

The mantra we use with our clients is "offer Rolls Royce quality at BMW prices." In other words, offer the best goods and services you know how to provide, all backed by the best guarantee you can think of (see last week's chapter) sold with the true desire to give value to your customers. Charge fair (not low) prices for your premium offerings. Done well, this creates a tremendous bargain (value proposition) for your customers. Find innovative ways to make said bargain known to your niche audience, and they might just flock to you.

OK, so you've followed our advice and aren't raking in the clams. Should you slash your prices? This knee-jerk instinct is dead wrong in most cases. Why? Every industry has its bottom feeders, those businesses whose one claim to fame is low prices. Shoddy products? Mistreated employees? Awful marketing? Yep. And that's OK, because these businesses are catering to those 14% of people who place price above all else. The moment you decide to compete on price, you will have literally stooped to that level. Take on the low price leader's one selling point and the result will be a bloody spiral of ever-lowering prices ending with someone falling into the bankruptcy abyss. Hint: Chances are excellent that the current low price leader will prevail.

Pricing itself is usually not the problem. The real problems tend to center around lack of confidence in the value being offered, self-esteem issues, and/or getting the message out to customers. In other words, pricing is very often a symptom and very rarely the disease. We'll talk about all of this in future chapters. Meantime, take heart: In all probability, you won't have to resort to slashing your prices in order to stay in business. In fact, you might need to raise them.

We leave you with a time-honored way to boost sales of the product or service you'd most like to sell: Offer good, better, and best versions, where the better version represents your ideal sale. Make sure to differentiate each tier by both offering (what's included) and by setting wide price points between tiers. Why? Some people can't or won't afford your middle tier. Offering a lower tier gives you a safety net that will capture at least some of this otherwise lost revenue. On the high end, some people will be perfectly willing to spend more money and your top tier gives them that opportunity. Most people will opt for your middle tier, which should be perfectly fine by you. This one simple tip is very easy to implement and extremely profitable.

Yes, there are exceptions to this rule. Yes, there are reasons why becoming the low price leader may be a good idea. Barring those rarities, however, do yourself a huge favor: Never, ever, compete on price!

WEEK 28
PUSH YOUR LIMITS

Anthony recently did something extraordinary: he began taking swing dance lessons and has expanded into tango and salsa. This might not seem so extraordinary to some or even most of you but it marks the first time in Anthony's 38 years on this planet that he decided to get over his fear of hitting the dance floor, master both of his two left feet, and find out once and for all whether his decades-old joke of "I'm poor and I ain't got no rhythm" was rooted in any kind of reality.

One hour of practice put that old saw to rest forever. Anthony discovered that he does, in fact, have rhythm and that he is quite capable of becoming a pretty good dancer. Better yet, mastering swing will help him learn other steps as well, thus broadening his horizons even further. During his second hour of practice, it finally dawned on Anthony that dancing is nothing to be feared. On the contrary, it's lots and lots of fun. It does of course help to have a great instructor.

This small accomplishment got us to thinking: How often do we shy away from opportunities or growth because we believe that we can't or shouldn't go there? How much does holding back cost in terms of personal fulfillment and business profits?

What limits have you imposed on yourself and/or on your business? Where did these limits come from and why? Are these limits real or imagined? How much profit and ease are you missing out because of these artificially imposed boundaries? What benefits might you get by pushing your own limits?

How do you begin to move outside your own comfort zone? The easiest way we've found to date is to just go for it. Swallow your fears, be prepared to swallow more than a little pride, and you may just surprise and delight yourself. The best part about exploring beyond your comfort zone is that one little success is all it takes to start you brainstorming other ways to grow and expand. For example, Jay had been resisting finishing a book he'd been working on for a long time. One afternoon, he returned home and polished it off in just a few hours. There's no way to know for certain whether the business deal he concluded that day helped him with the book, but there's no reason to doubt that either.

The lesson is simple: Just because you have been doing something a certain way (or not doing it as the case may be) for many years doesn't make it sacred, necessary, or even healthy for yourself or your business. Your business cannot grow beyond your own boundaries, meaning that you must grow if your business is to grow. Maybe you've been resisting hiring additional help because no one can do things exactly the way you do them. Maybe letting go of your need to have things done in such a special way will allow you to have more free time and grow your business by freeing you up to start a new marketing campaign. Maybe you're an artist who feels that art and business are like oil and water. Maybe letting go of this artificial boundary will allow you to use you artistic skills to grow a thriving business selling your art.

Brush your fears and trepidation aside and push your limits with all the gusto you can muster. The worst that can happen is that you'll reaffirm those limits, which isn't so bad because it's almost always good to be right. The best that can happen is that you will surprise and delight yourself as you discover skills and capabilities you never knew you had. Do this once and you may well be inspired to challenge yourself and grow in another area, then another and another. Where will this path lead? We have no idea. We can tell you that it will be lots of fun and possibly very rewarding in other ways.

Our chapters so far have focused on things you can do to bring people into your store or interest them in your services. You've read those articles over the past several months, taken some of our advice (hopefully), and customers are indeed coming into your store or contacting your business. Now what? Starting next week, we'll be presenting a series of chapters on marketing and sales with a focus on closing the deal once prospective customers contact you. If you like what you read, we encourage you to share the upcoming chapters with your employees and everyone who comes into contact with your customers. Stay tuned.

WEEK 29
THE THREE INGREDIENTS OF EVERY SALE

Congratulations! Your marketing efforts have paid off in the form of a prospective customer. Now what?

The bad news is that every prospect who departs sans purchase represents a failure to follow through on the interest built through your marketing. The good news is that there exists an extremely simple formula for qualifying your prospects and making more sales: want, need, and affordability.

Want. Does the prospect want what you sell? Want is an emotional response and human beings are emotional creatures. In fact, Anthony's research indicates that logic mainly exists to validate and rationalize our emotions. Think about your own logical processes and delve into why you made certain decisions and how you justify them. We'll bet that you'll find emotional underpinnings almost every time. You have therefore overcome a huge barrier whenever your prospect wants what you have to offer. If that want is strong enough, the prospect will do most of the work of establishing a need and figuring out ways to pay for it that could even include cutting back in other areas. If they don't want your wares, you are facing a steep uphill battle.

Need. Does the prospect need what you sell? There are two types of need. The first exists to justify and rationalize wants by forming perceived needs. For example, you may need transportation and may decide that you "need" the model with heated seats, navigation system, high-performance V6, etc. In this example, the need for transportation is the actual need while the need for luxury is the perceived need. Combine want with perceived need and you are well on your way to sealing the deal. And when you think about most marketing, isn't converting raw emotion into perceived need what it's all about? On the flip side, it is entirely possible to need something without wanting it. Going to the dentist comes to mind (with absolutely no offense meant to any dentists who may be reading this).

Many people would rather do just about anything other than going to the dentist. The alternative, however, is far worse. As an aside, we're seeing more and more dentists going out of their way to establish want by emphasizing how pleasant the experience can be.

Afford. Your prospect may be salivating at the idea of buying your product or service. She may even have built her perceived need into a matter of life and death. But can she afford it? The stronger the want and/or need, the more machinations prospects will contemplate in order to be able to make the transaction. Case in point: Anthony not too long ago performed numerous calculations under multiple scenarios to determine whether he could safely purchase his dream motorcycle (a low-mileage mint-condition 1993 Yamaha FJ1200). Ultimately, if your prospective customer can't afford to make the purchase, they won't. Period. Anthony got lucky.

Your job as a marketer is to establish each prospect's level of want, need, and affordability. A good series of questions to ask might be to establish what the prospect is looking for, the features they would like to have, and their budget. At that point, it's up to you to do your utmost to make the closest possible match. If the customer says they can afford $500, showing them the $2,000 model is a pointless waste of time. Showing them the $600 model that includes as many desirable features as possible is a much better approach. If the customer can't spend the extra $100, show them how your assortment of lower-priced models combines various partial combinations of features to determine which is most acceptable.

The lesson here is very simple: Establish exactly what your customer wants, needs, and can afford, then base your entire presentation around satisfying as many of those criteria as possible. Do that and your odds of making the sale go way, way up.

Notice the distinct absence of the word "close". The moment you resort to "closing" the sale, your odds of success plummet. Follow the formula outlined above and your customers will sell themselves. Your role is to facilitate their mental processes in conformance with their decision-making criteria. This makes you a friend and ally instead of a salesperson, which dramatically reduces both buyer's remorse and refunds.

Increased sales with more goodwill and fewer post-transaction problems. Does it get any better?

You have the raw formula. How you actually use it is a topic we'll begin addressing next week.

WEEK 30
THE POWER OF OPEN-ENDED QUESTIONS

How often have you heard the question "May I help you?" as you enter a place of business? If you or your employees regularly come in contact with customers, you all may have uttered that question hundreds or even thousands of times. The problem is that this question is closed, meaning that it only requires a one-word answer with no thought behind it. Hardly the way to engage someone who is trying to decide whether or not to spend money on what you have to offer. Remember that the key to obtaining market share lies in obtaining mindshare – in other words, people need to engage their brains before they'll break out their wallets.

The solution? Open-ended questions that require detailed responses and conscious thought to fully answer. In many cases, converting a closed question to an open-ended question is as simple as adding "Who", "What", "Where", "When", "Why", or "How" to the beginning. Thus, for example, "May I help you?" becomes "How may I help you?"

This extremely simple adjustment accomplishes three things.

- First, it signals the customer that you actually want to help them instead of simply exchanging formalities. Think about our customs and etiquette and you'll realize that most of it falls under "maintenance" behavior, which we engage in because we're expected to, not because we want to. Maintenance behavior is an obligation and that sentiment comes across loud and clear every time we hear it. Would you rather buy from someone who has to help you or from someone who wants to help you?

- Second, open-ended questions force your customers to think, which both embeds your business and your products and services in their brains and gets them started down the want/need/afford path to a successful sale.

"How may I help you?" "Who are you buying this for?" "How will you use this item?" All of those questions require thought to answer.

- Third (and most important), open-ended questions launch a dialogue between you and the customer, which magically transforms you from a salesperson trying to close a deal (take money from the customer) into an ally working to arrive a common solution (give value to the customer). Do you see the not-so-subtle difference here? Instead of selling something you want to sell, you are selling something your customer really wants to buy, which greatly reduces buyer's remorse and the refunds that come with that syndrome.

Skeptical? Jay was too when he first heard this many years ago. He decided to give it a try and hasn't looked back since. Yes, open-ended questions require more time and effort. Yes, this may reduce the sheer number of people you can "help" in a given day. Yes, you actually have to want to give value to your customer in order for this exercise to work to its fullest potential. But, hey, are these such bad things? After all, no matter your profession, you are in the business of serving your customers and the success of your business depends entirely on how well you accomplish that mission.

We encourage you to try a simple experiment: For two weeks, ask as many open-ended questions as possible, then tally up the results. All else being equal, you may just be pleasantly surprised by the results.

Next week, we'll discuss how to handle customer complaints and how they can actually benefit your business. We'll also discuss just how devastating poor complaint handling can be using an actual case study.

WEEK 31

CUSTOMER SERVICE: THE GOOD, THE BAD, THE UGLY

This chapter will doubtless seem rather more rambling than most; however, we hope you'll see, appreciate, and learn from the underlying message.

Anthony recently had his house painted. Part of the process required renting a paint sprayer to speed doing the bulk of the work. This seemingly simple task became an adventure that revealed both the best and the worst in customer service.

Marshall Kentish (painter extraordinaire) and Anthony reserved a sprayer from a paint store in town. Upon arriving to pick it up, they learned that it had accidentally been rented to someone else. The gentleman at the store was very apologetic and offered to let us rent the sprayer for free as soon as it became available. Try as he might, Anthony could not fault them. Yes, the store made a mistake, but everyone makes mistakes. The proprietor owned up to it by making a very gracious offer. The timing didn't work out for this project, but Anthony will gladly do business with that business again and refer others to them.

Marshall and Anthony next stopped at an equipment rental shop on Highway 66 right by the airport and picked up a sprayer. They lugged it home, got everything prepared, and fired it up only to discover that the machine was completely unserviceable. Ninety minutes after picking it up, they had the sprayer back at the shop after breaking it down, cleaning it, loading it, and driving back. The man behind the counter refunded only $18 of the $60 rental fee claiming that we had failed to return within 30 minutes (a physical impossibility) and that two people with a combined total of 35 years of painting experience didn't know how to operate the sprayer. He didn't even offer to show us how to adjust the machine. Anthony asked to speak to the owner. Refused. Worse, this man's tone and attitude were condescending and insulting from start to end. Anthony will never do business at that establishment again and urges anyone needing any kind of equipment to avoid heading out Highway 66 towards the Ashland airport at all cost.

Marshall and Anthony finally arrived at Ashland Rental on Highway 99 in Talent, Oregon. The store manager, Jim, was both friendly and knowledgeable — a true professional. He showed them his stock and let them test the machine before even loading it up. It worked perfectly and Anthony's house has never looked better.

The moral of this story is clear: Your customers are your lifeblood. You need them far more than they need you. There are lots of places to rent paint sprayers, buy food, etc. and most people only need one of anything at any particular time. Anthony probably won't need a paint sprayer for several years at least. Your average happy customer will tell three people about the wonderful experience they had at your business while the average unhappy customer will tell twenty. Anthony told thousands — including you.

Excellent customer service is one of the most potent forms of free or low-cost marketing there is since happy customers will be your loudest evangelists. Poor customer service is one of the fastest ways to destroy your business, taking your entire investment and possibly even your credit rating, house, etc. with it.

Believe it or not, complaints can actually lead to more business. Customers who experience satisfactory complaint resolution can actually be happier with a business than those who have never had a complaint. How is that possible, you ask? Complaint handling requires an investment of individualized time and attention, which is always a flattering experience on some level despite any frustration there might be. Besides, to err is human and everyone knows that. Think of the people who have wronged you and you'll realize that it's danged difficult to hold a grudge when the offending party freely offers to make things right. Their efforts show their good character and require no small amount of respect and admiration that might not have existed otherwise.

Don't get us wrong. We are certainly not saying that you should cook up excuses to make things right with your customers. We are saying that complaints can be your ticket to increased goodwill and profits or quite the opposite. It is up to you.

What is the secret to excellent customer service? Simple: Treat your customers how you would like to be treated in all situations. The moment you feel tempted to fire off a sharp reply to a request or a complaint, stop and ask yourself how you would want the situation resolved if the situation was reversed.

Even more on customer service next week. Until then, remember that applying the Golden Rule will yield more gold for you.

WEEK 32
THE X AND Y OF CUSTOMER SERVICE

Take a good look at yourself and any employees you may have who come into contact with your customers. This will likely be your sales staff but don't overlook any area of your company. Question: Is your X factor larger or your Y factor?

We're not talking about chromosomes.

Rather, we are talking about two very distinct personality types. At the most basic level, X people are all about command and control. They are the stereotypical "Do it because I say so" bosses, managers, and high-pressure sales people who tend to believe that some people are born to lead and others to follow. In other words, they are by far on the "nature" side of the nature vs. nurture question of human development and potential. By contrast, Y people tend to believe that everyone has a chance for greatness provided they are given the right environment. It should go without saying that Y people are strongly on the "nurture" side of the same question.

X people sell things. Y people create an environment that allows and encourages customers to make buying decisions. If you've ever been sold something, you had an X person helping you. If you bought something from someone and can honestly say you never felt like you were being "sold," you had a Y person helping you.

Many X people enter the sales profession thinking that closing the deal is all about leading and directing the customer to the sale. They may be right. After all, have you ever bought anything after a hard sell? Our guess is that you have. But how comfortable do you feel about the prospect of patronizing that business again and spending more money with them? Ah, now there's the rub.

Y people in the sales profession aren't really salespeople. They are guides, coaches, teacher, and facilitators. A customer walks in the door and gets guided to what s/he is looking for. The Y salesperson asks leading and thought-provoking questions designed to give the customer a space to talk about her or his needs, wants, and affordability. The salesperson teaches the customer about the available products such as features, limitations, warranty, pricing, financing, and so on. Combining all of these ingredients creates an environment that facilitates a decision to purchase — the best possible outcome. Second best, actually, because customers will remember the wonderful experience they had and (with a little help from you) become clients — that rare breed of customer who shops at your business again and again. With a little more nurturing, these same clients will tell others about your business.

Let us be perfectly blunt: Great marketing can and will lead customers to your business. One poor sales experience is all it takes to completely waste that effort. Consider the relatively low percentage of people who respond to even the best marketing (call it 5%) and you know you'll need to reach 20 more people to replace the one that just left your business in disgust. Even worse, this disgruntled almost-customer will tell 20 people about their rotten experience on average. You will therefore need to reach 400 people to replace the 20 you just lost. Multiply these numbers by every rotten sales experience that takes place at your store and we trust you'll agree that the results can be absolutely devastating.

On the flip side, nurturing customer relationships can yield breathtaking results. Here's the example we've used throughout this book: If a typical customer buys a $100 widget three times per year for 20 years, those purchases will add up to $6,000. If this customer refers three others, the total economic impact becomes $24,000. A bad sales experience could net you $100 at the expense of $23,900. If the disgruntled customer tells 20 people, your total loss becomes $125,900. All that to get someone to make one $100 purchase. Is it worth it? We don't think so either.

Take a good hard look at how your business treats its customers and ask yourself if you are marketing yourself into bankruptcy. It's that simple and that serious. As an aside, many X people who enter the sales profession leave because they eventually get sick of the mounting rejections. Sadly, by then, the damage has been done…

We have met plenty of wonderful X people as well as our fair share of Y people who aren't exactly on our Christmas card lists. All we are saying is that you need to take at least as close a look at your sales process as you do your marketing processes. The people handling your sales (and yes, that could include you) may or may not be well suited for the role. You may well have great people doing the wrong jobs. Make the appropriate changes and you'll be astounded at how your profits might jump. This is absolutely not about accusations or making character judgments. It is absolutely about making sure that the people responsible for the final step in the revenue generation process are the absolute best people for that specific job.

Boosting your profits dramatically could be as fast and easy as making a few simple changes in assignments.

WEEK 33
THE DEVASTATING IMPACT OF CUSTOMER COMPLAINTS

In the last chapter, we gave you some startling numbers about the amount of damage that customer complaints could be causing to your business. Those numbers assume that every customer with a problem will complain about it. The bad news is that the full truth is worse. Much worse.

Conventional wisdom holds that there are 25 to 50 customers with problems for every one who actually complains, making every complaint actually received only the tip of a very large iceberg. Assuming that every dissatisfied customer tells 20 others, you may well be turning away 500 to 1,000 customers for every one complaint that you are aware of. You read this correctly: For every one dissatisfied customer you know about, you could be losing over 500 potential customers. Can you afford those numbers? We didn't think so.

It gets even worse: Over half of the customers who contact your customer service department never report their most serious problems. Why? Because they believe that voicing their complaints won't do any good. Welcome to the age of "trained helplessness", where customers no longer even give you a chance to rectify a problem. The damage is still being done, but business owners are becoming less and less aware of it.

What are customers unhappy about? The bulk of their complaints are increasingly focusing on so-called "standard operating procedures" such as endless sales and marketing pitches. The never-ending barrage has trained customers to stop complaining and accept these situations as part of the status quo. Don't believe us? When is the last time you enjoyed a good meal and adequate personal space aboard an airliner? Our guess is that you maintained a stoic silence and took comfort from the fact that you landed safely. Do you ever have customers standing in line or otherwise waiting for assistance? If so, consider hiring more staff. The added cost of paying these employees will probably more than pay for itself in happy customers.

Here's a really depressing statistic: For every complaint about your standard business practices that you are aware of, there could be 30 to 50 unhappy people out there. Multiply that by 20 and you've got 600 to 1,000 people who may be less likely to do business with you. The implication is clear: More than a few businesses are quite literally their own worst enemies. Think about these numbers versus the effort that must be expended to make one new person aware of your company and lead them to buying from you and you will see that your worst competitor's best efforts cannot hold a candle to the damage you might be doing yourself.

The most shocking part about these numbers is that they are, if anything, conservative. Research has uncovered ratios as high as 2,000 unhappy customers for every known complaint. Wow!

Had enough bad news? We hope so, because the good news is that these numbers represent an amazingly potent opportunity for your business to differentiate itself from the herd with little more than innovation, dedication, and an extremely reasonable investment.

Got a standard business practice or policy that might be irking some customers? Read our chapter about re-serving your rights.

Here are some easy ways to buck the growing trend of trained helplessness and put the opportunity this phenomenon represents to work for your company:

- Train your employees to check in with your customers by asking questions like "Are you happy with your experience here today?"

- If a customer complains about one of your standard policies or procedures, be prepared to explain the rationale behind it. We hope for your sake that this process is truly critical for your business.

- Listen for thinly veiled complaints such as "I was standing in line forever" or "Customer Service never called me back." Comments like this will often get inserted into a conversation and are easily overlooked if you're not listening for them.

- The moment you receive a complaint, be sure to listen to what your customer has to say and ask them what you can do to make things right. You will be amazed at how trifling the fix usually is. Asking the customer how you can solve the problem empowers the customer, shows them that you genuinely care, and will usually cost less than any offer you might make.

- Make sure customers know that you take their satisfaction seriously. Solicit complaints and feedback in as many ways as possible. Tell your customers that you can only solve the problems you know about.

- Jump on, follow up with, and resolve every single complaint you get, no matter how petty it might seem.

Is doing all this easy, or is it easy? Many businesses today are looking for ways to cut their customer service to the bone and beyond. Bless those foolish, short-sighted penny pinchers, for they have created a tremendous opportunity for you.

Many (if not most) complaints surrounding "standard practices" focus around marketing. Next week, we'll show you why this represents a double opportunity for your business.

WEEK 34
REAPING THE DOUBLE WINDFALL

Customer complaints can wreak havoc on any business and can easily neutralize the best marketing campaigns. An increasing percentage of complaints center around so-called "standard business practices." That's the bad news. The good news is that you can use these facts to tremendous advantage. For example:

When it comes to customer service, are you and your employees experts in what your business does and sells? Finding people who know what they're talking about is becoming increasingly difficult, making those who do all the more refreshing. Do you ask open-ended questions designed to get the customer talking about her/himself or do you try to push products and services on them? Get customers talking about themselves and they will close the deal without you having to sell a thing. Better yet, remove buyer's remorse from the equation and the number of refunds you get will decline. Do you stand behind your products or do you restrict refunds and exchanges? Believe it or not, the more liberal your guarantee and refund policies, the fewer returns you'll get.

How about your marketing? Do you wax poetic about your company, your products, your services, your prices, you, you, you? Or do you build lasting relationships with your customers using a step-by-step process that turns leads into prospects into customers into clients into referral sources? Each step of this process must be all about giving value. After all, you can talk about how great you are, or you can prove it. Which carries more weight? Many customer complaints have to do with marketing. If you've ever deal with overly persistent telemarketers, you know exactly what we're talking about. What if these companies instead sent information of interest to you? Let's use this chapter as an example. Could Jay run weekly ads touting his skills and experience and exhorting people to engage his services? Sure. Would that approach be more or less effective for you than reading newsletters containing information that you can use to improve your business?

Are you seeing a common thread here? We hope so because the simple truth is that your business is not about you. It's about your customers. If you go out of business, customers will simply shop elsewhere. You're the one who will be in a world of hurt, not them. The secret is therefore to always err on the side of your customers. Place yourself and your employees in your customers' shoes and learn to constantly ask what you would want to happen were the situation reversed.

The Golden Rule states that you should treat people the way you want to be treated. If you are applying the Golden Rule in your business then you are already light years ahead of far too many of your peers. That said, let us suggest the New Golden Rule, which states that you must treat people the way they want to be treated. Do that and you will virtually eliminate customer complaints. Do that and your marketing will be all about your customers. Right there, you will have overcome the all-too-prevalent perception among consumers that "they, (businesses), don't care about me, they just want my money."

The sheer number of businesses that have lost sight of treating customers like the lifeblood that they are means that you have a real opportunity to stand apart from the crowd. Look for the book *Guerrilla Marketing in Action* in 2007. This book is a follow-on to the video by the same title produced circa 1993. Guess what: Every single business featured on that tape is still in business today and going strong. The one common thread binding these disparate entities is their unwavering dedication to their customers. You get our point.

This is not to say that you can't or shouldn't play favorites. Take a good look and you'll probably find that you're getting 80% of your business from 20% of your customers. Treat these people like family. Treat those who buy less like royalty. Treat everyone else like honored guests.

Place your customers' needs and wants ahead of your own and your needs will be richly taken care of. Place your needs ahead of your customers' and you will go wanting. It's that simple.

Great customer service and customer-centric marketing need not be expensive. It need not be difficult, complex, or overly time-consuming. It must, however, come from the heart. Master both and you will reap not one but two very profitable windfalls. That's a promise.

The ability to place yourself in your customers' shoes depends to a great extent on your level of knowledge about what you are selling. Becoming an expert in your products and services will give you deep insights into your customers' needs, wants, and budgets. This will help you close more sales. The same holds true for your employees. A little investment in training can pay off handsomely. We'll talk about that next week.

If you want to know more about the power of giving as a way to increase your own abundance in work and life, we cannot recommend *The Power of Giving* by Azim Jamal highly enough. You can find this book at Amazon.com or at your favorite bookseller. This book is proving to be a tremendous help to us and it can help you find innovative ways to reap the windfalls described above.

WEEK 35
ALL ABOARD THE TRAINING TRAIN!

If you think education is expensive, try ignorance.

What a wonderful bumper sticker and how appropriate it is for every facet of life, including our businesses!

The simple fact is that nobody knows everything. The odds are therefore very good that your business has several knowledge gaps that could be costing you a pretty penny in lost profits and missed opportunities. If your business has employees, that might be a very good place to start searching for those gaps. For example, a well-known auto muffler chain was converting about 75% of people who phoned the store into customers. They implemented a half-day phone training policy and forbade anyone lacking that training from answering the phone. Their conversion ratio shot up into the high 90% and has remained there ever since.

Assuming that each employee costs $25 per hour, the trainer $500, and that there are 10 employees per store brings the total cost of each 4-hour training session to $1,500. If the average sale is $100, each store will reap over $2,000 in increased sales for every 100 phone calls. Substituting the above numbers with your actual figures will show you how much benefit you can expect from training your own employees — and yes, that could include you as well.

Today's world of globalized trade and cutthroat competition has many businesses scrambling to cut costs at all cost. If you've read any of our previous chapters, you know that we are all in favor of reducing costs because that can be a great way to boost profits. For example, if your net profit margin (what's left over after paying all of your expenses) is 5%, then lowering your costs by 5% can literally double your profits overnight. We stand by that example because we've seen it work in plenty of businesses.

The thing to remember is that all expenses are not created equal. Extravagance and inefficiency are two categories of outlays that you must eliminate immediately if not sooner. Investments, however, are a totally different story.

If spending $1,500 can yield a 20% higher conversion rate for the foreseeable future, then not spending that money becomes the waste.

You and/or your employees are the public face of your business and can literally determine whether your business thrives or folds. Over the past few weeks we've shown you just how much damage poor customer service can cause. We've explained how the best salespeople are coaches and guides who are experts at what they sell and who know how to interact with your customers on their terms. These skills require training to develop, nurture, and refine. You therefore have a choice:

- Convince yourself that you and your people already know everything you need to know. You may be right, but ask yourself if your business is truly functioning at peak efficiency and profitability. If the answer is no, then training might just be the investment that changes this situation.

- Insist on hiring only "perfect" people. To err is human, meaning that the perfect employee simply does not exist. Yes, you must have high standards; however, setting the bar too high can slow your business down and cause you to miss opportunities for growth. It's rather like restricting air flow to an engine, which will never produce peak power under those circumstances.

- Take a thorough intellectual survey of your business to find your strengths and weaknesses, and then invest in training to plug those gaps. Find the best people you can and train them in how your business operates, which we guarantee is at least a little different than any other business on the planet.

We both urge you to select the third option. Do so with the idea that everyone has an equal capacity for greatness in her or his own way and that everyone has the innate desire to show off that greatness. Do so from a place of wanting more for your employees than they might want for themselves. In other words, create an environment where you and your employees can shine and shine you will. Creating this environment will foster passion and loyalty and will boost your bottom line by leaps and bounds.

The bad news is that this scenario is not as idyllic as it might sound because you will find some bad apples in the form of people who can't, won't, or don't mesh with your business for whatever reason. The good news is that creating a system for investing in your employees will help you discover and weed out those who aren't a good fit far more quickly, easily, and with less rancor than ever before.

Above all, approach your training as an opportunity to grow your business instead of as a necessary evil. The destination isn't the point; it's the journey that is all-important. You're on this journey whether you like it or not so you may as well make the best of it. Ongoing training is one of the most powerful ways to get the most out of your journey.

Hey, if you think education is expensive, try ignorance.

Next week: The real meaning of the word "work".

WEEK 36
"WORK" REDEFINED

Imagine two identical piles of dirt that must be moved an identical distance. Person A uses a kiddy shovel and takes all day. Person B uses a tractor and moves the entire pile in one scoop.

Question: Who did more work?

At least 80% of the people we ask say Person A. We believe this occurs because people tend to equate "work" with "effort". Physics, however, defines work as results. Both people, therefore, did the exact same amount of work. The difference is that one struggled while the other obtained results with ease.

Society conditions us to define work as struggle. We are expected to spend 40+ years in a job with the goal of amassing enough money to live out our few remaining years in some semblance of comfort before departing this world. Talk about slavery! Even worse, self-employed people who struggle in their businesses are even more deeply indentured. A worker can quit and find a new job whenever s/he wants. Walking away from a business isn't that easy.

We bet some of the people you know succeed at everything while others crash and burn no matter what they try. Luck? Does God, the Universe, or karma favor some over others? No. Everybody has the same potential for success, the same chance to accomplish anything they want in life. The key lies in our beliefs. The physical world we see, smell, hear, touch, and taste is nothing other than the sum of our perceptions filtered by our beliefs. We're sure that you've heard the maxim that 20 people witnessing the same event will provide 20 different accounts.

If you believe that success requires working a job for forty years, then you will get a job. Forty years later, tired and spent, you'll have achieved your result: a short time of relative leisure before death. Die too soon and you'll leave behind some of the resources you spent your entire life creating. Live too long and you'll expend your resources and die with nothing. How's that for depressing? The mechanics of this phenomenon are quite simple: Whatever one invests energy in grows. Invest energy in the idea that work equals struggle and struggle you will.

What about you? If you think that you "work hard" or feel that you can't or shouldn't do something because it's "too hard", then you define work as effort. We've lost count of the entrepreneurs we've met who feel absolutely overwhelmed because they're struggling just to stay afloat much less thrive. These unfortunate souls desperately want more from their businesses but dread the thought of thrashing even harder in the murky waters of their own making.

If this describes you or someone you know, then we have wonderful news: It doesn't have to be like this. There is a better way. Today we challenge you to stop defining work as effort and embrace the scientific definition of work as output. Quit focusing on the effort and start focusing on the results you want. Do that and you will struggle a lot less while getting far better results far more easily. And why not? If you're in business then your business should be serving you, never the other way around.

Freeing yourself from the "work equals struggle" trap is as easy as divorcing yourself from the idea that struggle is necessary and that the way you have been doing things is the only way there is. This can be difficult because nobody wants to admit being wrong. We see it this way: Your current methods have served you admirably because they delivered you to this exact point in your life. Sure, they may need some updating but that doesn't make you wrong. Think about your childhood. Were you wrong for using diapers and crawling on the floor or did you simply outgrow those habits? There is nothing whatsoever wrong with growth.

Next, examine your goals and seek the easiest ways to accomplish them. Be creative! Having defined your destination and the easiest way to get there, proceed in small simple steps being absolutely sure to reward yourself for every single step. The destination is nice, but never forget that life is a journey that you can choose to enjoy… or not.

The payoff can be nothing less than spectacular. A contractor Jay knows tripled profits while working 25 fewer hours per week. A healthcare franchisee who worked with Anthony expanded by 80% while trimming 15 hours from her weekly schedule. Another businesswoman experienced greatly reduced stress levels just by carving out one hour of personal time every morning. There is no reason why your results can't be just as good or even better.

Define work as results and seek ways to obtain the results you want with ease and you'll soon be struggling a lot less while reaping far more abundant results and enjoying life's journey far more. That's a promise.

WEEK 37
BRIDGING THE GAP BETWEEN ART AND BUSINESS

"I'm an artist, not a businessperson!"

Are you an artist struggling to make it in business? We've heard a lot about the perceived divide between art and business. In fact, Anthony's coaching career began when he produced a series of DVDs aimed at helping new authors publish and market their books more effectively. Those DVDs also led to Anthony meeting Jay. The rest, as they say, is history.

Today we'd like to proffer the idea that selling one's art is part of the artistic process. Think of creating the art as assembling the pieces and making the sale as breathing life into your creation. After all, what is a book without readers, a play without an audience, a painting without viewers, or music without an orchestra but a meaningless ensemble of tangible or intangible artifacts? Art exists to convey a message — an impossible task unless you present it to the world.

Some artists avoid money because they believe they might somehow cheapen their work by making it commercial. A noble sentiment; however, we have two questions: First, are you an artist? Are you fulfilling your life's calling or dharma by creating your art? If you answered yes to both questions then you are bringing abundance into the world by following your life's calling. How can you be undeserving of receiving just as much abundance as you give?

Strip money of its connotations and you'll discover nothing but a universal medium of exchange. Earning money through your art gives you the needed resources to continue fulfilling your dharma and thus completes a closed circle. Avoid earning money through your art and your efforts will be constantly stymied as you struggle to feed yourself while finding time and energy to be artistic.

We're not saying that you need to sell out. On the contrary, you must find those few people who will truly connect with the message contained in your art and no one else's. If you've been following our chapters, you'll know that we're talking about nanocasting. How does one nanocast? One word: marketing.

Remove the fear and mystique surrounding marketing and you'll find that it is nothing but the act of spreading a message. Ponder the many ways in which you consciously or unconsciously radiate messages every single day and you'll see that you're already marketing.

The trick is to refine your message and deliver it to the right people.

If you're like most artists we've met, you're feeling torn between itching to get going and dreading the journey.

No problem.

Begin by researching successful artists to determine who you can compare and contrast your art against. Gather as much information as possible about these people. For example: Where do they sell their work? Who exactly buys it? How much do they charge? How do they describe their work? Who has reviewed their work? Remember that information is power. The more information you have, the better prepared you'll be to carve your own niche in the art world. If you're an author or artist in any medium that works with other professionals such as agents, distributors, publishers, retail outlets, wholesalers, printers, photo labs, galleries, etc. then take the time to learn who the players are in your industry, what they do, and how they work.

Fellow artists can be one of your best and worst sources of information. Our advice is to seek out people who are where you want to be in terms of sales, fans, etc. Learn from them for they have walked the path you aspire to walk and can offer guidance and encouragement every step of the way. Most importantly, they have succeeded and know that it can indeed be done. Don't get mired in the angst and misinformation floating among other emerging artists. This may sound a little harsh but then again you wouldn't dream of learning to fly an airplane from anyone but an expert… or so we hope.

Having amassed this information, your next step is to decide whether your commitment to selling your art matches your interest. If not, then stop now and come back if and when that changes. Life is too short to waste on anything you aren't truly committed to. Finally, decide exactly how much money, fame, etc. you'll need in order to deem your efforts a success. Far too many people miss this simple question: "How will you know when you've won the game you're preparing to play?"

At this point, STOP and reward yourself for having taken these first steps. Rewarding yourself at every step is crucial for your future success.

Your next step is to balance your goals with available resources. We'll cover that in next week's chapter.

Don't consider yourself an artist? We've got news for you: Everything we said above applies just as well to your business.

WEEK 38
BALANCING INTEREST AND COMMITMENT

Last week we mentioned that one of the first things for any entrepreneur to decide is how you'll know when you've won the game you're about to play (such as starting a new business.) For example, football has rules about the methods and time constraints for scoring points. At the end of the prescribed period, the team with the most points wins. You must define your goals in equally specific terms. For example, "passive income of $5,000 per month within one year" is very specific.

Defining specific goals is a mandatory first step and laudable in its own right. The danger is that saying you want to achieve something is a far cry from actually doing it. The things you say you want to do and accomplish are the things you're interested in. The things you actually invest time and resources in are the things you're committed to. If your interests and commitments match, then all is well. The problems begin when commitments don't match interests. Think about it: If you say you want to build a passive income of $5,000 per month and spend your time sitting around dreaming about how you'll spend all that money instead of taking steps to earn it... See where we're going?

Thankfully, reconciling interests and commitments is very easy.

Begin by writing down your total net monthly earnings on a sheet of paper. Now itemize each of your expenses by category (food, shelter, utilities, debt, entertainment, etc.) making sure to include everything, even incidentals and investment contributions. Subtract your expenses from your total earnings. How much is left over? On a side note, if this number is zero or less than zero, then you may be using debt and/or draining assets to maintain your lifestyle — an extremely dangerous habit.

Look at your schedule next. A week has 168 hours, 56 of which should be spent getting 8 hours of sleep per night, leaving 112 waking hours. Add up all of the time you spend working, playing, commuting, bathing, eating, waiting in line, etc. On another side note, if your time commitments exceed 112 hours per week, then you are not getting 8 hours of sleep per night, which could be causing or contributing to any number of health problems.

In theory, all unallocated funds and time are available for any purpose you choose. Question: Are these resources enough for you to achieve your goal? If so, great! But if not, then you need to start making some choices.

Can you divert funds and time away from other pursuits towards this goal? For example, could you eat out less often to save money or shop at different hours to save time? If so, then making these changes will help you on your way. If not, if you are truly locked into your financial and time constraints, is there some lesser goal that you can achieve on your way to the bigger one? We have yet to see anyone unable to make at least some progress.

Are you willing to make whatever changes you can for the sake of achieving your goal? If so, go ahead and make them. If not, that's OK too. In this case, however, you must adjust your interests to suit your commitments. This may mean deciding to build only $1,000 of passive monthly income in the first year to help you take the next step. You could also decide to give yourself two years to achieve the whole thing. The bottom line is that you must make adjustments because you can't or won't act on your stated goal for whatever reason. Your commitment does not match your interest.

Keep in mind that this has nothing whatsoever to do with judgment or blame. It has everything to do with balancing your interests (what you say you want) with your commitments (what your actions create for you) so that you can decide and act on the things that matter the most to you. Life is way too short to waste doing anything else.

This lesson applies to any goal in your business or personal life because each is a series of choices and compromises. Want to launch a new marketing campaign? If so, how will you measure its success and what are you willing to do to accomplish that success? Want to hire some part-time help to reduce your workload? If so, can you afford it or make changes to be able to afford it?

Next week: How would your life and business change if you could never fail, if everything you did was absolutely 100% successful?

WEEK 39
SUCCESS GUARANTEED

Last week we challenged you to ponder how your life and business might change if you were certain that you couldn't fail, if you knew that everything you attempted was guaranteed to succeed 100%. What would you do differently? What risks would you take? What journeys would you embark on? In short, how would your material, mental, emotional, and spiritual outlook change and how would those changes manifest themselves in your daily lives? Take a few moments to let this question seep in and see what answers come to you.

Having pictured your ideal life or business, my next question is: What's stopping you? Why aren't you achieving the results you want? Where are the obstacles on your road to success?

The answer is that each of us is conditioned to expect a certain amount of success. We carry built-in limits that specify how materially wealthy we can be, how much happiness is enough, and the extent to which we can follow our dreams. Exceed those limits and a correction takes place. Imagine a thermostat set to 70 degrees. On a hot day, the temperature in the building rises to 71. Sensing the heat, the thermostat kicks in to cool things down. On a cold day, the thermostat comes on to heat the building when the temperature drops to 69 degrees. The thermostat is therefore "hunting", or moving up and down while maintaining the average temperature.

Look back at your life and we'll bet that you'll see periods of extraordinary (relative to the average) periods of wealth, happiness, business profits, etc. You will also see periods of hardship, struggle, and seeming inability to make anything happen no matter how hard you try. Average these two out and you'll probably arrive at an amazingly level average. That average is your comfort zone. Think about that comfort zone and how faithfully you've stuck by it and you'll realize that you haven't failed at all. Quite the contrary, everything you've done has been absolutely perfect for maintaining that safe, navigable average. Congratulations! You have been 100% true to your commitments and have reaped 100% success from those efforts.

It gets even better: Your 100% success rate with your life or business to date means that you can create any kind of success you want just as successfully. That's right: All of your trials, tribulations, and hardships mean that you can have anything you want. Hey, if a computer can execute Program A flawlessly, it stands to reason that it should execute Program B just as effectively, right? The program may be flawed, which could cause crashes and other problems, but the computer is executing that program faithfully right down to the errors — it can't distinguish between good and bad programming. We would be more than a little scared of a computer that didn't follow its programming, even if that meant avoiding an error.

Fix the programming and the computer will run it perfectly. The same analogy holds true for you. If you don't like the life or business you have, then all you need to do is change how you define success and everything else will change accordingly. Changing a definition is easy — and therein lies the problem, for this change is, literally, unbelievably easy. The inability to believe just how simple this change is means that actually doing it often requires months or even years.

Changing your definition of success is as easy as 1-2-3:

- First, own the fact that you and you alone are responsible for your life, your business, and everything in it. In this context, "responsible" literally means "able to respond". You alone have the ability to respond to what you want in your life and business. Ability is another word for power. Own your power.

- Second, define exactly what you want materially, emotionally, and spiritually. The only way to get where you're going is to know where that is.

- Third, get used to the idea that there is no such thing as failure. You have achieved absolutely everything you were truly committed to. Change your commitments and you will achieve them with equal success.

How would your life and business be different if you were guaranteed 100% success? It's a trick question. They already are. The moment you commit to the success you are interested in (see last week's chapter), you'll start receiving it.

Next week: Preparing for success.

WEEK 40
PREPARING FOR SUCCESS

You've raised your personal success thermostat per last week's chapter and understand that you can expect 100% success from your commitments. You've even taken steps to align your interests with those commitments. Free of your old limits, you're waiting patiently for the good stuff to rain down on you... but nothing's happening.

Why not?

Pretend you have a toddler who is accustomed to drinking from spill-proof plastic kiddy cups. One evening, he decides he really wants to drink like a grown-up. You unscrew the cap and give the child his first "big boy" cup of water. Within moments the cup crashes to the floor spraying water everywhere. My guess is that you'd respond by cleaning the spill before going into the kitchen to refill the cup. After all, the child is just learning; besides, we all knock over the occasional glass.

You return to see Junior lunging from his highchair and grabbing your much larger water glass. You'd snatch it out of his hand as quickly as possible... wouldn't you?

Why? First, Junior just demonstrated his inability to handle a small plastic cup. No way can he manage a big glass. Second, the glass could break and give the child a nasty cut. The lesson is obvious: As a kind, loving adult, you won't set Junior up for failure by giving him more than he can handle. Well, dear readers, life works exactly the same way. You will only get as much as you can manage at any one time and not a bit more. Your inability to manage what little you do have lies behind your business difficulties and any want for money, happiness or other blessing. Until you learn to manage your current situation, you will not see any improvement. Furthermore, as bad as your situation may be, imagine how much worse you'd feel if you suddenly got everything you ever wanted – and lost it all.

My guess is that would cut you pretty deep – just like the shards from the broken glass could cut Junior.

The Universe is the kindest, most benevolent, and loving entity there is. Don't believe us? Consider the staggering odds against your being born in the first place. Now consider that there has never existed a being just like you in the entire eleven-billion (11,000,000,000) year history of this Universe, nor will there ever again once you leave this plane of existence. You are a priceless jewel in the grand scheme. It would be a tragedy of cosmic proportions for you not to live up to every ounce of your potential yet that is exactly what will happen because the Universe will never set you up for failure by giving you more than you can safely manage.

If you want to increase your physical, mental, emotional, and/or spiritual wealth, then you must begin by learning to manage what you have. Live within your means. Account for every penny of revenue and expenses. Knock out your debt. Build your savings. Commit to doing this and find creative and meaningful ways to reward yourself at every step of the way, and you will get a tantalizing taste of what's to come.

Create management systems that can scale to accommodate any level of wealth and you will find yourself rewarded with more abundance than you dream possible. This abundance may or may not come in the form of money; however, if you are living your life's purpose or dharma, then you will be truly wealthy in life and business. We define our own states of wealth as having the freedom to live, love, and laugh while making a powerful difference in the lives of everyone we meet. How do you define wealth? There is no wrong answer.

If there is one thing that unites all humanity, it is that our time on this planet is limited. If there is a hereafter (as we both firmly believe there must be), then one can argue that our performance in this lifetime sets us up for the next. And if we only get one spin on the crazy merry-go-round of existence? Either way, you're either growing or dying. Want proof? Think back to a college or high school course you took where you got good grades. If you had to take the final exam over again right now without studying, what kind of grade would you get? Did you say "not so good?" Why? Because you stopped growing in that subject and consequently your knowledge and expertise in that area began dying. Same with your success: If you want to keep succeeding, then you need to keep growing, which means you need to keep learning. Begin by learning to manage what you have and more will follow. That's a promise.

WEEK 41
CLEARING YOUR SLATE

Christmahanukwanzaa heralds the end of the year. It is a time for celebrations, gifts, and looking to the future. It is also the time when most businesses (probably including yours) are getting ready to close the books on the year in anticipation of starting fresh on January 1. This year, we'd like you to go one step further by taking a long look at your business over the past year and asking yourself some probing questions.

Here are just a few:

Has your business served your needs and enabled you to live your ideal lifestyle, or has your life revolved around your business?

Are each of your business processes truly necessary or do you find yourself doing some things because you've always done them? Of the necessary processes, how many of them are running at peak efficiency and how many could be streamlined? How could this streamlining occur?

Do you have the information you need when you need it and does this information contribute to your decision-making process? If not, where is the chain broken? Do you need to purchase new accounting software, create customized reports, or rely more on the numbers instead of gut instinct?

If you vanished tomorrow, would your business keep running smoothly, sputter, or fail altogether? Why? How can you create a business that stands on its own two feet instead of sitting on your shoulders? Far too many entrepreneurs reach retirement and try to cash in their businesses only to realize that they themselves are the business, which lacks any real value beyond them. What this question really boils down to is: Is your business building equity that you can cash in later or do you need to think of other ways to fund your retirement?

Is your business self-sustaining or is it draining resources from loans, capital, personal infusions, etc? If your business needs additional resources to remain open, are you a start-up? Is this business a hobby where you don't really need or want the money? Or are you struggling? If so, why? What can you do differently to ease this situation?

Have you examined your products and services to determine your most and least profitable lines? Would eliminating the under-performers boost your bottom line? Remember that profit, not revenue, is what matters.

Are you protected in the event of calamity? For example, do you have enough insurance to guard against disasters? If your business requires your presence in order to run, do you have enough disability insurance to replace your income if you are no longer able to work?

Is this business fulfilling or allowing you to fulfill your dharma or life's mission, or is it limiting or even preventing you? Our time on this planet is limited and the two words no one should have to utter in their final moments are "if only".

Do you have a solid, well-defined marketing process that converts leads into prospects into customers into clients into referral sources? Do you see your marketing as a strategy where every tactic (Web site, brochures, signs, etc.) has its defined place and role? Or do you think of marketing in terms of "things to do" with no unified purpose?

We are sure that you can think of many more questions to ask yourself. We hope you take the time to answer them fully and honestly because doing so will paint a broad picture of your business's strengths and weaknesses.

This is the season for celebration. List all of your successes and make sure you celebrate them with your loved ones and with the people (such as your employees) who helped make them possible. You deserve to reward yourself for every single accomplishment.

This is also the season for reflection and looking ahead. List all of your business's problem areas and your ideas about why those problems exist. Examine each problem from cause to process to effect. Then celebrate again! Why? Because you have successfully identified things to change or eliminate altogether and have learned and grown as a result. Each item on your list represents an opportunity for you to innovate and experiment, a chance for you to recapture the thrill of discovery you undoubtedly felt when you launched your business.

Identifying your strengths and weaknesses will help ensure that your business thrives in the new year. It is not about finding fault or assigning blame. It is all about clearing your slate of anything that might be holding you back from the success you want and deserve.

WEEK 42
MAKING (AND KEEPING) YOUR RESOLUTIONS

How many of us wake up on January 1st bound and determined to turn over a new leaf? Of this number, how many are still at it more than a week or so later? Our guess is that the second number is but a tiny percentage of the first. What happens? Where does the moral and motivational fervor we feel on December 31st go and why does it dissipate so rapidly?

One word: homeostasis.

Your body and mind are designed for sameness. Humans love stability in everything from our body temperature and heart rates to our habits. Change, no matter how welcome or how badly needed, is calamitous. Think back to some of the major changes you've experienced in your own life and ask yourself just how stressful those situations really were. People don't like change and our sub-conscious minds will do everything in their power to maintain the status quo no matter how awful it is. Turn over that new leaf and your body will detect the change and take steps to remedy it. Chances are that you won't even realize it's happening until it's too late. This is no accident. Your subconscious mind is constantly doing everything in its' power to keep the homo sapiens (you) in stasis (in your comfort zone). This is an inexact definition of homeostasis but is close enough for this discussion.

> - First, define your goal right down to the who, what, where, when, why, how, and so what.
>
> - Second, define easy steps that you can take each week. Having done that, forget everything but the current week's step. Next week isn't

here yet, so worrying about that step is pointless. Last week is done and gone. Focus solely on this week. Do you see what you've done? Your huge lofty goal has just become manageable in a way that lets you see results very quickly.

- Third, accomplish your milestone for the current week.
- Finally, decide in advance how you're going to reward yourself for achieving your week's milestone. This reward need not be costly or complicated. It must, however, be creative and meaningful to you on more than a superficial level.

The good news is that you can hot-wire this inner programming and make whatever changes you want in your life or business using a simple 4-step process:

These easy steps render even the most complicated goals simple by letting you bite off one small piece at a time. Best of all, you get to celebrate and feel great about every single little piece. Life is a journey. You may as well enjoy it.

You can apply this process any way you like. Want to start a new business? Grow your existing business? Lose weight? Hire additional help? Get a professional certification or degree? Prepare and file your taxes? You can do it, and this process can help because it tricks the mind into thinking that things are remaining stable when tremendous changes might in fact be happening. Dive into a pool and your entire body will feel the shock. Go in slowly and you'll hardly notice the cold. The same logic applies to this four-step process.

What do you want to accomplish this year? We're certainly not suggesting that you stop making New Year's resolutions. We are suggesting that you take a little time to help guarantee your success. And why not? Don't you deserve to succeed?

Be good to yourself and your life and business will be very good to you. Follow this four-step process and you will accomplish more in less time and with more joy than you ever dreamed possible. That's a promise.

WEEK 43
JUMP-START YOUR DAYS

If you're looking for an easy way to greatly reduce stress while boosting your productivity then today is your lucky day. We're going to share a technique called the Hour of Power, which was developed by our friend Azim Jamal (www.azim-jamal.com), an internationally recognized speaker and author.

Begin by going to sleep one hour earlier than you normally do. If your days are anything like ours were before hearing about Azim's program, then your last waking hour is pretty much a waste because you're already shutting down for the night. Quit fighting your tiredness and get to sleep. Make up this lost hour by waking up one hour earlier than you normally do. Chances are that you'll wake up more refreshed, meaning that your day is already off to a better start.

Begin your day by sitting in quiet contemplation or meditation for 20 minutes. Use this half-waking time to let your mind free-associate as you ponder the day ahead. What do you need to do today? What challenges or obstacles lie before you? How can you be even more effective than you already are in marketing, management, communications, etc? Are there any personal issues that could hamper your ability to complete your business and other obligations for the day? How can you balance your work and personal lives more effectively? How can you derive joy from the day to come?

Follow your quiet time with 20 minutes of physical exercise. Aerobics, tai chi, calisthenics — what you do is unimportant so long as you get your blood moving. This simple step will cause your body to burn up to twice as many calories per day as you would without exercising. Increasing your body's metabolism will fill you with energy and eliminate any sluggishness. Your health and fitness levels will improve. This feeling of well-being will help motivate you to achieve whatever you need to achieve that day and work towards longer-term goals. Never overexert yourself and always seek professional medical advice if you have or develop any health problems, especially if you haven't exercised in a while.

Spend the last 20 minutes of your hour reading something uplifting. What you read isn't important. What is important is that you enjoy reading it and leave feeling better than when you started.

We encourage you to set aside your own Hour of Power at least four times per week and hopefully every morning. The clients we've shared this with have reported lower stress levels, increased energy, improved moods, greater clarity, and higher productivity. They also report that seemingly intractable problems suddenly seem more manageable.

This method is particularly effective for anyone who is working towards a major business or personal goal or who is leaving their comfort zone for any reason. Remember that your mind and body are trying to maintain the status quo and will do everything they can to revert you to your old habits. Taking the time to center and energize yourself each morning will go a long way to keeping you on track.

The Hour of Power has an additional benefit: It gently forces you to examine your day and your life in general. Dr. Wayne Dyer asks if we are living ten thousand days or if we are living the same day ten thousand times. This question takes on new significance — and urgency — when one considers just how fragile life is and how none of us knows when our time will come. Anthony got a reminder when he and his wife found their dog Shidoni lying dead on their laundry room floor. Shidoni had been alive and well that morning, and all signs pointed to a sudden passing with no warning whatsoever.

The end can come at any moment for any one of us. How will you use your remaining time on this planet to grow your business and personal abundance and build a lasting legacy? The short answer is that you can do all of this and more by living your life consciously — and the Hour of Power can be a powerful tool to do just that.

L'chaim. To all of our lives.

WEEK 44
DO YOU NEED HELP?

Business is booming. You're running out of hours in the day. Customer service is slipping. Sleep is becoming a precious commodity. Leisure is a four-letter word. It's high time to find some good help.

Or is it?

As we've said, many entrepreneurs open their businesses only to discover that the goods or services they provide are almost an afterthought compared to the many tasks required to keep the business open. For example, making and selling candy at a candy store is only a tiny fraction of the many things that have to happen on a daily, weekly, and monthly basis to keep the doors open. Overwhelmed, the proprietor hires someone and heaves a huge sigh of relief. This person is a marvel who tackles all assignments with a smile. Over time, the employee's task list grows and grows until one day she can't take any more and quits. In this situation, the business's demise is usually not far off. Burnout is one of the leading causes of business failure, above and beyond money issues.

On the other extreme, growing companies sometimes hire far too many people due once again to poor planning or to basing their work estimates on the slowest person on the team. Idle employees are a tremendous waste of time and money.

The first example typically applies to smaller businesses while the latter more often applies to larger businesses such as growing corporations. Some of the dot-com companies we worked with were shining examples of runaway growth.

What should you do if you're contemplating growth?

Begin by taking a long hard look at your business and examining every single process that takes place therein. For each process, ask yourself if it's truly necessary or if your business can survive (or even thrive) without it. Next, ask yourself how you can streamline your business-critical processes. The goal here is to tune your business up to peak efficiency and profitability before growing it. Having a solid foundation will help you identify whether you do in fact need the help and, if so, where exactly you need it.

Having ascertained that you do need help and where you need it, your next task is to create a job description against which you can screen potential employees and measure their performance once they come aboard. This description must be detailed enough to give both you and your prospective employee a very clear idea of what's expected yet not so comprehensive as to be stifling.

Keep in mind that planning your growth, selecting your new employee, and training that person will require an investment of time and money. These resources that may be in short supply and you may be tempted to sidestep the preliminaries. Don't succumb to this temptation. Instead, think of the process like a vaccine — a short, possibly painful experience that will prevent much larger problems in the future.

One of two things will happen as a result of your self-examination: You may find that you can shave so much time off your schedule that you really don't need the help. If so, your business will be far healthier and you'll be saving tens of thousands of dollars per year, money that can go right to the dear old bottom line.

If you do need help, you will have an excellent idea of where you need to grow. You will be able to select, hire, and manage someone with a clear purpose. Even better, your new employee will know exactly where s/he fits in and how s/he is contributing to the overall effort. That knowledge is one of the biggest motivators there is, one that is many times more powerful than a mere paycheck.

Either way, your business will be on a solid foundation. You wouldn't dream of adding another floor to a building with a crumbling foundation, so why grow your business on an equally shaky footing? Any problems that exist with your business today will grow with every new employee and will become harder and harder to correct.

Prune the deadwood from your business and plan for intelligent growth, and your business will be on the path for long-term health and vibrancy. Fail to plan and you are sowing the seeds of your business's eventual demise. Which outcome do you want for your business?

OK, so you've done your planning and pruning and are itching to start interviewing people. Not so fast, because you haven't yet identified your ideal candidate — a process that is very similar to identifying your ideal customer. But that's next week's topic. Meanwhile, here's a homework assignment for anyone considering expanding their payroll: If you have not done so, read *The Emyth Revisited* by Michael Gerber. While you're at it, read *Nickeled and Dimed* by Barbara Ehrenreich for some great ideas on how not to manage your employees.

GUERRILLA MARKETING SUCCESS SECRETS

WEEK 45
WHO SHOULD HELP YOU?

In the previous chapter, we wrote about the need to make your business as efficient as possible and to create clear job descriptions prior to seeking additional help. Remember that every employee you take on without performing these two all-important tasks only makes fixing any problems your business currently has that much harder.

Who should fill the opening you just created and defined?

Scan the want ads and you'll see all sorts of requirements from personality type to years of experience at a particular function. Some employers insist on drug and/or background checks. Are these factors really important? How can you know?

Begin by examining any regulations governing your industry. What certifications, clearances, and screening does the law require for your vacant position? Next, will the employee be handling any sensitive or mission-critical tasks such as money, accounting, or working at customer locations? If so, you may wish to consider background checks and perhaps bonding them against any accident or malfeasance. Next, does this position absolutely require any specialized knowledge or training?

Years ago, Anthony saw an ad for a technical writer with experience documenting rail cars. He has training in mechanics, hydraulics, pneumatics, etc. — all of the components found in a rail car — but was rejected because he'd never documented an actual rail car. The ad continued running for months. It is certainly possible that rail cars possess some arcane technology that Anthony is not aware of. Barring that, the experience requirement was just plain silly and prevented the work from getting done.

If you followed the steps we outlined in the last chapter, then not bringing on help is probably costing you more than hiring someone. You need to balance your need for speed against the need to find the perfect match. How?

We have already expounded about the need to define your ideal customer. We encourage you to do the same now for your ideal employee. Take some time to write down all of the traits you could possibly want in the perfect employee. Be as specific as possible. For example, if you'd like them to have five years of experience working on rail cars, write that down. Let your mind run free as you do this because creativity is a powerful tool when unleashed.

Once you've created this list, it's time to buckle down and refine it into the actual job requirements. This is mostly a process of elimination. Begin by deleting absolutely everything that is or could be discriminatory such as age, race, and gender. If needed, seek expert guidance to make sure that you are not creating potential problems for yourself. Next, ask yourself whether technical skills or personality take precedence. If the employee will be working behind the scenes (such as on a production line), then technical skills may be more important. If s/he will be working with customers, vendors, etc. then personality may be the larger consideration. Chances are that you'll need some combination of the two. Remember that "marketing" is all contact between everyone in your company with everyone outside your company and plan accordingly.

Your laundry list should have lots of scribbles and deletions on it by now. If you think this resembles the process of finding out what makes your business unique (see the chapter about finding what makes your business special), then you're absolutely right.

Go back over your list one last time, stopping at every item to ask yourself whether it's truly necessary (and if so, why) or optional. Once this step is complete, you're almost done. Your final step is to cross-check these requirements against both your list of things that make your business unique and your definition of your business's ideal customer. If your list of employment requirements complements your business's uniqueness and meshes well with your ideal customers, then rejoice for you have just defined the perfect employee.

If not, edit the employment requirements list until it reaches this point. Never forget that your business exists to serve your needs, not the other way around. Your employees work to serve the business's needs, not the other way around. Thus, by extension, your employees are serving your needs. As the chief said when Anthony joined a volunteer fire department many moons ago, "you are joining us; we are not joining you." Of course, in a perfect world, working in your business will satisfy your employee's needs as well.

This process might seem long and involved, and it is. On the other hand, when you consider the potentially disastrous results of hiring the wrong person for the wrong job, we think you'll agree that taking the time to plan and define the help you need and who should fill that need is a very small investment to make in your ongoing success.

Next week: Quantity and quality

WEEK 46
HOW MUCH IS ENOUGH?

So far in this series on hiring, you've defined a job position and your ideal employee candidate. Your next step is to define how much work you expect from this person and how much you're going to pay them.

Setting clear performance expectations is essential for ensuring that your business is getting value from everyone who works there. You need to define both how much work gets done (quantity) and how that work should be done (quality) in no uncertain terms. Remember that the definition of "marketing" is all contact between your business and the outside world. You've invested a lot of time, energy, and money growing your business to this point and cannot afford to erode any of that hard-won progress.

Clearly defined expectations give both you and your employee an objective benchmark against which to judge performance. If the employee meets those expectations then all is well. If s/he does not, then either you made a mistake somewhere or your employee is not right for the job. Firing someone is an extremely difficult thing to do under the best of circumstances. Being able to demonstrate that you have an objective standard and that the employee consistently failed to meet that standard will go a long way towards easing this process for everyone concerned. Having clear expectations will also help protect you against a costly wrongful termination lawsuit.

Spell out exactly how much work you expect from each employee every week or even every day and exactly how you will measure the quality of that work. Make sure that every employee agrees to this in writing and keep that agreement on file because you will need it in the future. Keep in mind that you are no less infallible than anyone else and encourage your employees to inform you if they deem your standards unrealistic. It is entirely possible for you to expect too much or even too little.

It may seem like we're discussing standards from a punitive angle but this is not the case because standards work both ways. If you hire someone who consistently performs above and beyond what they are expected to do, then you can use the same benchmark to justify rewards such as bonuses, raises, and promotions.

How much are you willing to pay for this performance? Low wages might seem tempting but may come with hidden costs in the form of reduced performance and increased turnover. Can your business afford less output or quality? Can it afford the extremely high cost of employee turnover? A minimum wage worker earning $7.50 per hour in Oregon costs a bare minimum of $3,750 to replace (just over 25% of their annual salary). Do you really want to waste that kind of money? You read that correctly: Every employee who leaves your business costs you about 25% of their annual salary or more.

We suggest that you approach your wages the same way you approach your pricing. You may remember our 80% rule of thumb where you price yourself at 80% of the difference between the lowest and highest prevailing prices for similar goods and services. Likewise, find the lowest and highest prevailing wages in your area for similar jobs and consider offering 80% of the difference between the two. For example, if the job pays between $8 and $12 per hour, consider offering $11.20 (80% of the $4.00 difference is $3.20, which you add to the $8.00). This is a very rough guideline that you will need to adjust based on your individual situation and goals but it does give you a good starting point.

Should you offer more or less? That's a complex question. Offering more can attract better employees who will stay with you longer and do better work, which can have dramatic effects on your bottom line, to a point. Whatever you decide, never make the mistake of thinking that lower wages equals less cost and higher profit. It's just not that simple.

Clear performance expectations and decent wages are critical for attracting and retaining employees who will add value to your business and themselves but there is a third ingredient we have not covered yet: management. That's next week's topic. In the meantime, if you have or are considering hiring employees, we again urge you to read *Nickeled and Dimed* by Barbara Ehrenreich for some great lessons on how not to manage employees.

WEEK 47
THOUGHTS ON MANAGEMENT

Once upon a time Anthony worked in several hardware stores in San Francisco, two of which stand out for their exceptional management practices.

At one store, the owner constantly complained about how slow business was and daily berated his managers (Anthony included) for failing to place the many notepads, tools, etc. at perfect right angles on the glass countertop that he insisted on keeping spotless. Training was non-existent as were benefits or decent wages. Turnover was extremely high, especially among the more qualified people. Customer service was spotty at best because hardly anyone knew the inventory or how to help people solve their many problems from replacing sink washers to wiring telephone extensions. That store limped along for many years and finally folded. It was sad driving by the empty building that once hosted Anthony's first real job after high school.

The last hardware store Anthony worked at sells many of the same products but that's where the similarity ends. Each employee is responsible for their department (paint, plumbing, electrical, glass, etc.). New employees are assigned to senior employees in a department, fully trained, and promoted when the senior person leaves. The person in charge of each department handles ordering, inventory, customer service, pricing, cleanup, the works. The master schedule rotates everyone through their departments and the cash wrap, ensuring enough people at the registers while giving everyone plenty of time to manage their own departments. Everyone is an expert in their area and refers customers to each other when a question exceeds their knowledge. Living wages, benefits, and paid vacations are the norm. A surprising number of that store's employees have been there well over a decade. Customers and workers are on a first-name basis. That store has been thriving year after year and recently expanded.

Here is the single most powerful secret you'll ever learn about managing people: The more you put into them, the more you'll get out of them. Here are just a few examples of what we're talking about:

- Openly communicate your business's goals and standards. Everyone wants, even needs, to belong to something. Give your people something to belong to and to strive for.

- Whenever possible, hire people who are just a little too junior for the position, mentor them, and watch them grow.

- If you expect your employees to give you their full-time dedicated efforts, then give them the resources (pay, benefits, etc.) to do it. Forcing someone to work two or more jobs in order to afford food and shelter forces them to give you less than their best efforts.

- Set very clear expectations about the quantity and quality of work that must occur and hold everyone to the same standard (including yourself).

- Make your employees experts. Encourage them to share that expertise with each other and with your customers.

- Always treat your employees the way you would like to be treated. Fail to do so and, well, when the cat's away...

- Never tolerate drama. You are not in the therapy business. Well, maybe you are, but you get our point.

- Push your people to excel by keeping your standards high. Anything worth doing is worth doing well.

- Mistakes happen to the best of us. If an employee makes a judgment call that proves wrong, heck, at least they took the initiative.

- Most employees are decent hardworking people; however, there are exceptions. Firing people sucks. The distraction and resentment wrought on an entire team by one bad apple sucks even worse.

All this is a very long way of saying the obvious: Be firm. Be fair. Be a leader. If you can't or won't do that, then chances are very good that hiring employees could cause more harm than good. But if you can, then your business will see

- Be candid about the state of the business. Your employees are literally selling part of their lives to you and this lifetime may be the only one we get. They deserve nothing but the truth. Make them part of the solution. The intelligence and creativity at your disposal will amaze you.

- Recognize that your workers may have more detailed knowledge in specific areas than you do. We never saw Captain Kirk tell Scotty how to fix the warp engines.

- Praise publicly.

- Punish privately.

increased productivity, morale, job satisfaction, and customer satisfaction while seeing less turnover, fewer complaints, and sharply reduced losses (we'll talk more about loss prevention next week). All of this adds up to one thing: Higher profits — the reason you're in business in the first place.

WEEK 48
LOSS PREVENTION

You may want to keep a bottle of antacid nearby as you read this.

Dishonest employees are the single largest source of business losses due to theft and fraud, eclipsing shoplifting, vendor fraud, and other external sources. 75% of employees have stolen at least once and 50% of employees steal more than once. Employee theft costs up to 3% of a company's gross sales (one study even goes as high as 6%). Assuming a net profit margin (what's left over after paying all expenses) of 5% of your gross sales, then employees are walking off with up to 60% or even 120% of the total profit (3 is 60% of 5). The United States Department of Commerce estimates that 30% of business failures are caused by poor hiring practices. The average family of four spends over $400 per year because of inventory theft, which is only one of the many ways employees can steal from a business.

This is not a drill, people, nor is it a scare tactic. No, dear readers, this one means you. If you have employees, then chances are excellent that your business is part of these statistics whether you want to believe it or not.

Feeling a little ill yet?

The good news is that there are some simple things you can do to greatly reduce (and possibly eliminate or prevent) internal loss in your business, none of which require a "get tough" attitude. Getting tough won't work because it will expose the inevitable loopholes in your system as clearly as stars on a cloudless night and give your employees all the motive they need to exploit them in a classic example of "F--- me? No, f---- you!"

Good management is the single largest factor behind preventing internal theft. We covered this in the last chapter when we advised you to be firm, be fair, and be a leader. It's easy to steal from the jerk boss. It's much harder to steal from one's own team. Forge a tight-knit team and never be anything less than honest with them and you'll solve most of the problem in addition to reaping the other benefits we mentioned in the last chapter.

Education is also key to reducing losses. Your employees know how much money is coming in and how little of that makes it into their paychecks. What they may not know is that 95 cents of every dollar your business earns gets spent before you get to keep any of it. You need not make business majors or accountants out of them; that said, we encourage you to practice an "open book" policy so your employees can see the money going out just as easily as they see it coming in.

Implement a few commonsense controls such as:

- Have your accountant examine your books regularly and have another random accountant audit them from time to time.

- Match every line of every packing list with every item you receive and report overages or shortages.

- Take regular inventory and match that against your orders and receipts. Keep a closer eye on especially tempting items.

- Periodically remind employees that theft hurts everyone, including themselves, whether or not they get caught.

- Study other prevention methods in use by other businesses in your industry and decide which ones are appropriate for you.

- Be alert for any sudden changes in employee behavior or circumstances.

- Remember that if it seems too good to be true, it could well be. Some of the worst theft comes from the employees who seem to be going the extra mile and then some, such as working long hours, never taking vacations, etc. We don't mean to imply that your best employee is your worst enemy. We are telling you to remain alert.

- Become a technophile. A well-managed computer can be your best friend in many areas, including loss prevention, the key words here being "well managed." Are you seeing a theme here? We hope so.

The best hiring and management practices can't prevent everything but they can reduce problems from potentially fatal to the business to occasional annoyances. Should you ever find a problem, respond appropriately and then put it behind you. Never succumb to the temptation to take out your justifiable shock and anger on your other employees because doing so may just cause more headaches than it solves.

Above all, don't be paranoid. Be the best leader you know how to be, use your head, and you'll have little to worry about. Yes, we are harping about this.

You may notice that we haven't covered external losses such as shoplifting. We did this for two reasons: First, external losses are a much smaller problem. Second, the same commonsense methods you implement to prevent internal theft will help alleviate the external problem as well.

WEEK 49
THE JOYS OF TECHNOPHILIA

Can you keep a secret?

We're technophiles.

In case no one else has done so, let us have the honor of welcoming you to the information age where s/he with the most bytes wins. Like it or not, technology is here to stay. We urge you to embrace technology and take full advantage of its amazing power to (among other things):

- Keep you in touch with your customers through regular emails, a Web site, chat rooms, blogs, etc.

- Create marketing collateral such as catalogs, postcards, and much more.

- Track inventory and customer purchases.

- Monitor your business's finances and financial health.

- Handle your payroll.

- Deliver training to employees and customers.

- Simplify ordering.

- Speed design and other services.

- Allow you to simulate virtually any scenario without committing resources until you're ready.

- Control climate, access, security, and more.

- Copy, print, and fax.

- Build products.

These are just a few of the ways in which computers can revolutionize the way you do business if they haven't done so already. One machine costing less than $1,000 can do everything we've described above and much more — too much more for us to list. In fact, the single biggest challenge all technophiles face lies not in finding and processing vast quantities of information but in deciding which tidbits in the flood merit attention and which can — and should — be ignored.

We use our computers to write books (including this one), manuals, letters, exchange email, create 2D and 3D art, process and edit audio and video files, watch movies, listen to music, keep ourselves on schedule, handle our finances, connect with friends, book travel, track inventory, market our products and services, play games, and more. Anthony even met his wife Robyn in an Internet chat room.

Our guess is that you're either a technophile like us (in which case we're preaching to the choir) or a technophobe who thinks that we're crazy for putting so much stock in a machine. There are lots of reasons to fear computers. Viruses and hackers can corrupt and steal your data. More and more life-impacting decisions are being made by machines. Have you ever been approved or denied for credit? Chances are increasingly good that a machine made that decision with no human intervention whatsoever. To this all we can say is that the machines are only as good as the people using them. There is nothing inherently good or evil about a computer any more than there is about any other imaginable implement.

How does one begin the transformation from Luddite to full-fledged techno-geek? Very gradually. Begin by purchasing a computer. Most computers available today are more than capable of handling your current needs with plenty of room to grow. Next, transfer one of your manual processes over to the computer. It helps if this process is one you find tedious and/or boring. The initial learning curve might be steep and painful but you'll soon find yourself getting more and more comfortable with the computer and should start noticing some benefits like time savings, increased accuracy, etc.

From there, find a separate task or function related to the one you just computerized and see how you can link the two of them. Having just mastered one small use for your new computer, this second frontier will be far easier to cross. Keep going, task by task, function by function, until your business is reaping the full benefits of this new technology.

It is often said that work expands to fill a vacuum. Save a bunch of time by switching to a computer and you'll find ways to spend even more time at work. Well, the choice is yours. You can choose to enjoy the time you save out side of work, invest it in growing your business, or by finding new ways to keep yourself busy. It's up to you.

Using a computer wisely can save you a huge amount of time, money, and aggravation. Using a computer unwisely can lead to some pretty nasty problems. Either way, however, a tectonic shift is occurring in how we work and play and how we measure success, all thanks to technology. You can choose to evolve or you can choose to be left behind. The question is no longer just about getting ahead; it's about maintaining the status quo as well. You've worked hard to build your business. Embrace technology and help it thrive.

WEEK 50
WHAT'S YOUR EXIT STRATEGY?

You know as well as we do that your involvement with your business is anything but permanent. Circumstances such as age, health, or the simple desire to do something else will eventually separate you from your business. If you've come this far without having the end in mind, then you need to start asking yourself a very profound question: What is your exit strategy? When the time comes, how will you leave your business behind? Will you sell it? Shut it down? Deed it to your heirs?

If your plan is to sell your business then you need to ask yourself the following question: Are you building equity in your business or are you merely generating cash flow? The answer can have significant ramifications.

Imagine starting a business and working it all your life with the idea of selling out come retirement time and living on the proceeds. Now imagine your shock and devastation at learning that you can't sell your business for anywhere near what you thought it was worth because you failed to build equity. This real-world horror story happens to far too many entrepreneurs after a lifetime of toil. Not quite as bad, imagine thinking you can sell Business A to buy Business B or fund some other endeavor only to be rudely surprised.

Building equity in your business is the process of building lasting value that can be transferred to anyone once you're done with it. One of the key elements in building value lies in creating and refining products, methods, and systems that don't rely on specific people to carry them out. Fast food franchises are the perfect example: Anyone can prepare a Big Mac anywhere on the planet with perfect consistency. Both Jay and Anthony have eaten Big Macs on several continents as part of a long-running experiment and we have yet to tell the difference. If Ray Kroc was the only person on the planet who could prepare the perfect Big Mac, then he could never have spawned the worldwide McDonalds franchise. Sure, his burger joint could have earned a pretty penny in his day, but it would never have built the same kind of lasting value.

Think about your business. If it depends on you plying a unique skill or trade, then you may not be building much equity. Case in point: A few months ago we were considering purchasing a résumé-writing service with the idea of using it to expand our coaching services. We did a little digging and found that the owner was doing most of the work while farming a little out to a handful of longtime contractors. This business was based on referrals, meaning that her customers liked her unique writing style and approach, which no one else can ever duplicate. There is no way that business was worth its asking price, which the broker derived using standard valuation models that are incapable of taking such factors into account. It would be both easier and at least 99% less costly to start our own résumé-writing service. We still feel sorry for that business owner.

You can avoid this trap very easily by taking a good hard look at your business and asking yourself whether its value comes from what it does or from who is doing it. If the former, then you may indeed be on the path to building equity that you can later cash out to fund your retirement or other pursuits. If the latter, then you are probably generating profits while building little or no lasting equity for you to sell.

It's perfectly OK for you to be in a business that is generating cash flow but no equity. The key is for you to realize such a business for what it is so that you won't base your plans around value that won't be there when the time comes. In this situation, consider setting aside a portion of the profits in investments, savings, annuities, etc. that will be there when the time comes. The time will come. That much is certain.

Never forget that your business exists to serve you, not the other way around. It would be a tragedy for your business to stand beside you only to abandon you when you need it the most.

We urge you to seek expert advice from several sources to help you determine which path you are on and how best to use that to your advantage because leaving your business should be just as exciting and joyful as starting and operating it. You deserve nothing less.

WEEK 51
ON WOMEN IN BUSINESS

We have worked with and for many great people of both genders. In this chapter, Anthony is going to talk about three of the women who stand out when he looks back at his career to date and offer a few thoughts. He has changed the names but the stories are real.

In early 2003, Anthony decided to create a series of DVDs to teach authors how to market books. His concept was to film different segments in different outdoor locations and to have a woman on camera with him for a series of conversations about each topic. His friend Catherine volunteered for what they anticipated would be a few hours' shooting.

They anticipated wrong. Filming required three long days of traveling from location to location in hundred-degree heat. At each location, they unloaded, set up, calibrated equipment, prepped cue cards, and rolled tape, trying their best to look bright and perky despite the sweat pouring down the insides of their black shirts. Part of the filming called for aerial footage. Throw a pair of wings and a propeller on a preheated oven and you've got a pretty good approximation of what flying the plane was like.

Despite the hardship, Catherine remained friendly and supportive throughout, even intervening when Anthony and the cameraman got into a disagreement. Her dedication, creativity, and support kept them going and gave rise to not one but two finished products.

This would be a great story if it ended there but it doesn't. With Catherine's encouragement, Anthony contacted Jay to ask him to endorse the videos. That snowballed into Anthony creating a DVD product for Jay using the lessons learned from those first projects with Catherine. Even better, Jay encouraged Anthony to start his own coaching practice and made him both a Guerrilla Marketing speaker and Certified Guerrilla Marketing Association Business Coach.

More than once Anthony wanted to fold and accept defeat but Catherine's many donated hours and steadfast dedication kept him going because there was no way he could quit on her. She still reminds him of the work he's doing and her conviction that he is achieving great things. But for Catherine's professionalism and unwavering faith, you probably wouldn't be holding this book in your hand right now.

Anthony once worked for a dot-com company as a technical writer. He's accustomed to and adept at extracting information from recalcitrant engineers but this nut was particularly tough to crack. The fact that his immediate supervisor shared the prevailing seat-of-the-pants attitude didn't make matters any easier. Diane, the VP of Operations, was having none of it. She transferred Anthony's group to her department under Tina, the QA Manager.

Things changed awfully quickly. QA demanded full documentation for each new release as part of their testing. Operations used those documents to double-check everything before pushing the new code live. This begat a formalized process that covered every new release from conception to live implementation, resulting in improved quality and efficiency company-wide.

We've heard it said that men tend to be interested in carving out territory and status while women gravitate toward nurturing. While men think in black and white, women think in many shades of gray. Catherine's example is one of pure nurturing. At face value, Diane and Tina's example seems to be about power and status with Operations battling Engineering for turf and control within the company. But is it really about that? We think not. The guys in Engineering were hell-bent on progress. The women in Operations supported that progress 100% but wanted to make sure that everything happened in an orderly fashion to avoid chaos and disruption. Thus, they too were coming from a desire to nurture the company.

Men are powerful creatures. None of us would be here but for an unbroken chain of men who have successfully dominated predators and enemies since the dawn of time. The male drive to dominate has kept our species alive. Nature's rules are very clear: those creatures unable to rise to the top of their ladders are eliminated, through premature death and/or the inability to reproduce. Might makes right. Or so Anthony once thought.

Many years ago, another woman introduced Anthony to the idea that power can also come from vulnerability — that being able to say "I love you" to someone might require more fortitude than simply moving in for the kill.

We saw an ad from the 1950s showing a man wearing a shirt and tie lounging in bed with his arms behind his head as his kneeling wife sets a tray on his lap. The slogan read "Show her it's a man's world." Cigarette ads circa 1970 targeted woman saying, "You've come a long way, Baby." Was that ad a response to the civil rights and feminist movements of the 1960s? If so, the implications are frightening.

In the opinion of these two men, our gender has made the tremendous blunder of mistaking nurturing and vulnerability for weakness and inferiority. Today, we see women competing for equal treatment by emulating male tactics with the result that women are increasingly suffering and dying from traditionally male diseases caused by stress.

Our small examples highlight some of the differences we see between men and women. We don't for a moment believe that men and women are equal because we are physically, biologically, and psychologically different. That said, we don't for a moment believe that men are superior to women in any way or vice-versa. Each gender has its strengths and limitations that together have helped humans flourish.

Both of us owe parts of our careers to some amazing women. Both of our personal lives are blessed by each of our female friends. It is our hope that mankind will learn to appreciate and value the quiet nurturing power that is womankind. Taking a look at the state of our male-run world, we hope this change occurs much sooner than later.

WEEK 52
HAVE FUN!

Can you believe that this missive marks our fifty-second chapter? We thought it would be appropriate to celebrate this milestone and your progress by offering a quick recap of some of the many topics we've covered:

- Never forget that marketing is far more than advertising and PR. Marketing encompasses all contact between anyone inside your company with everyone outside your company. If someone see, hears, smells, feels, or tastes something and it's coming from your company, then you're marketing whether you know it or not.

- We discussed the idea that time is life itself. You can invest time earning money to market your business or you can bypass the money and go straight to the marketing. Marketing need not be expensive, time consuming, or difficult to be complex.

- Remember to build a marketing process that uses a series of gentle steps to convert leads into prospects into customers into clients into referral source and don't forget to enlarge the frequency, size, or networking potential of each transaction in addition to seeking new customers.

- Practice your public speaking skills. They really will serve you in good stead.

- Always err on the side of the customer. Replace "no" with "yes". Offer ironclad guarantees that take the uncertainty out of buying. Strive to bring every customer to a state of bliss so that they will sing your praises to the heavens and insist that everyone they know do business with you. Build and maintain an ongoing dialogue by asking your customers what they want and then consistently delivering more.

- Resist the urge to diversify. It is better to do one thing extremely well than to do a bunch of things half-heartedly.

- Find ways to market your business by giving value instead of by seeking to take from your customers. You can waste a lot of time and money telling people how great you are or you can win lifelong clients by proving it to them from the very beginning. The word "free" can be one of your most important allies in this endeavor.

- Your business exists to serve you, not the other way around. Achieve and surpass your goals with ease by breaking large goals down into easy weekly steps and making sure to reward yourself for taking each step.

- Bring your business to peak operating efficiency before trying to grow it, especially when considering hiring employees. If you do plan to hire additional help, take the time to define a clear job description, who best to fill it, and how to track performance. Communicate all this to your employees and give them the resources they need to give you their best efforts.

- Take heart in the fact that there is no such thing as failure because you are always 100% successful at whatever you commit to. Balance your interests with your commitments and you will never experience defeat again.

- Learn to manage what you have before expecting any more. If you want abundance, manage what little is yours to manage now so that you won't squander the riches when they come.

- Take one hour each morning to exercise for 20 minutes, read something uplifting for 20 minutes, and sit in quiet mediation for the remaining 20 minutes.

- Know that nothing is ever permanent and the time will come for you to leave your business. Plan your exit in advance so that you can reap the maximum reward for your work. Whatever you do, always remember

> that work equals output, not the effort required to generate the output. Nothing in any of my columns requires much effort. On the contrary, my goal is to show you just how easy running a successful business can be.

We have one more bit of wisdom to pass on before closing out this year: HAVE FUN! Take your business seriously but not too seriously. It's relatively hard to go wrong with anything you've set your mind to doing. It's almost impossible not to succeed at something you love doing.

Please write to us and let us know how you've used these past 52 chapters, the results you've achieved, and anywhere you're experiencing difficulty. The sooner you get your letter to us, the sooner we can help you, so write it up and mail it off. Then get ready because Year Two of *Guerrilla Marketing Success Secrets* starts... now!

GUERRILLA MARKETING SUCCESS SECRETS

NEED MORE HELP?

JOIN THE GUERRILLA MARKETING ASSOCIATION

85% of businesses don't last more than 5 years and only 4% are making a sizable profit after that period. The good news is that you can get an edge that helps you become and remain profitable and that keeps you thriving by joining the Guerrilla Marketing Association (GMA) today. The GMA may well be the most important "secret weapon" you have ever come across.

GMA members have direct access to Jay Conrad Levinson, the Father of Guerrilla Marketing and the bestselling author of the *"Guerrilla Marketing"* series of books with over 14 million copies sold in over 40 languages. He is the creative force that made household names out of the Marlboro Man, the Pillsbury Dough-boy, Allstate's good hands, United's friendly skies, and the Sears Diehard battery.

As a member, you will also receive the monthly *Guerrilla Marketing Insider* report filled with over 20 cutting-edge marketing tips that are new, actionable, and either extremely inexpensive or free. Each report includes videos with top marketing people.

You will also receive a one-hour weekly real-time telephone coaching and Q&A session with Jay Conrad Levinson and recognized experts and coaches, all of whom are there to give you immediate answers.

Grow your profits by joining Certified Guerrilla Marketing Association Business Coach Anthony Hernandez each week for LIVE guided discussions on a wide range of marketing topics.

Visit the Guerrilla Marketing Association site daily for the Guerrilla Marketing Tip of The Day, which takes less than one minute to read and which can have a permanent impact on your business. You'll also receive the *Guerrilla Marketing Weekly Intelligence* report via email.

Post questions and get personal answers from Jay himself or one of his hand-picked Guerrilla Marketing Association coaches, usually within 24 hours. Some of these experts charge $1,000 per hour for their services, which are included in your Guerrilla Marketing Association membership at no extra cost.

Visit the Guerrilla Marketing Association today at:

www.GuerrillaMarketingAssociation.com

today to sign up. You can't afford not to.

NEED EVEN MORE HELP?
HIRE A COACH

You've read the book, made some changes, and realize that you need to make more. Try as you might, you can't bring yourself to do what you know needs to be done. Maybe you're feeling tired, depressed, and/or burned out. No matter what your situation, remember that you're doing your level best to achieve your goals and dreams. Whether it seems like it or not, you are on the right path. You may need a little help and that's perfectly OK because no one exists in a vacuum.

Working with a coach is one of the most powerful ways for you to transform your business, even possibly your life. A coach gives you the individual attention and focus you need to:

- Define your goals
- Create a series of easy steps
- Accomplish each step
- Reward your progress

If this sounds good to you, then Anthony invites you to contact him to see whether coaching is right for you. His clients consistently report amazing progress and he'd love to help you do the same. He take a big-picture approach that looks at your life and your life's goals and creates a balance where your business can contribute to those goals instead of keeping you from them.

Need some help moving forward in a non-judgmental and supportive environment? If so, and if you are truly committed to achieving your goals and dreams, then please contact Anthony. Drop him an email, visit his Web site, or give him a call. There is never any obligation and you have absolutely nothing to lose. Here's how to reach Anthony:

- **Web site:** http://www.coachanthony.com
- **Email:** anthony@coachanthony.com
- **Telephone:** 1.415.786.2081 (Anthony's direct mobile number)

RESOURCES
BOOKS, CDs, AND VIDEOS

Books:

• *The Enlightened Savage: Using Primal Instincts for Personal and Business Success* — www.theenlightenedsavage.com

CD audio:

• *Guerrilla Marketing 101 Bootlegged** (by Jay Conrad Levinson) — www.gm-101.com

DVD video:

• *Guerrilla Marketing 101: Lessons from the Father of Guerrilla Marketing* (by Jay Conrad Levinson) — www.gm-101.com

NOTES

NOTES

NOTES

NOTES

NOTES